Then Comes the Baby in the Baby Carriage

Charles S. Mueller

SAINT LOUIS

Copyright © 1994 Concordia Publishing House
3558 S. Jefferson Avenue, St. Louis, MO 63118-3968
Manufactured in the United States of America

Library of Congress Cataloging-in-Publication Data.
Mueller, Charles S.
    Then comes the baby in the baby carriage / Charles S. Mueller.
        p.XXcm.
    ISBN 0-570-04666-1
    1. Child rearing—Religious aspects—Christianity. 2. Parenting—Religious aspects—Christianity. 3. Family—United States—Religious life. I. Title.
HQ769.3.M84 1994
649'.1—dc20   94-25525 CIP

1 2 3 4 5 6 7 8 9 10   03 02 01 00 99 98 97 96 95 94

Then Comes the Baby in the Baby Carriage

CPH Books by Charles S. Mueller

ALMOST ADULT
THE CHRISTIAN FAMILY PREPARES
FOR CHRISTMAS
LET'S TALK
SCHOOL-DAZED PARENTS

*To the many effective parents who willingly
shared their understanding of what it means to
be God's person in families today.*

May we learn as well as you have taught.

Contents

Introduction:
The Search for Effective Parents

---◆---

Our children are the yardstick by which we will be judged most frequently. If they are our legacy, let's invest in them.
    —*A North Carolina Mother*

The decision to write a book about effective parents and how they do their parenting was quickly and easily made. As far as I was concerned, it was time the real experts had their day. High time! Psychiatrists analyze and psychologists dissect parents anew each publishing season, many writing good books. Educators and sociologists take their turns at explaining the parenting process too. Pastors, counselors, sociologists, columnists, and various public figures add to the mountain of advice. But there has been a deafening silence from those who are doing what others report. Until now. In this book effective parents have their day. They will be allowed—better yet encouraged—to speak. Want to hear one?

This is being written late at night while I wait up for my oldest daughter to get home from going to the movies with a group of friends. Isn't that part of it?

An effective counterpart chimes in from four states away:

Our family is neither perfect nor ideal. However, if we can just figure what God wants us to do, it may become both.

One more: *It's about 5:30 a.m. right now. My three-and-a-half-year-old woke me with his coughing on his nightly trek into our bedroom at 4:30 a.m. He's asleep now. I'm awake. I think I'll write.*

Those three voices illustrate some of the reasons I've fallen in love with these uncommonly common people. They not only tell it like it is, they live it that way, too, confronting the problems, the puzzles, and the possibilities of parenting—each day. Let's listen again:

- *We find parenting to be one of the **most** challenging things we have ever done.*

- *Ruthie and I realize that the **most** important thing we do in this life, outside of following Christ, is raise our children. In every decision, large or small, we try to take the children into consideration.*

- *Parenting has turned out to be the **most** difficult and demanding task I have ever performed. It is also the **most** rewarding. My children are young. I have no way of*

*knowing whether I am doing a good job
or not. I pray every day for their welfare
and happiness.*

I surfaced effective parents in different ways.
I just came upon some of them as I bumped along
in life. It doesn't take long to spot them. All you
have to do is listen.

To make sure I had genuinely effective parents by the hand, I also measured them against the
witness of Scripture and the views of current family authorities. After a while I reversed the process:
I measured the family authorities by my newly discovered effective parents. How many did I just
happen upon? A hundred parents or so. Most
came paired, as a team. But not all. There were
many single parents. *Great* single parents!

My prime source for finding effective parents
was parish pastors. Who knows better what effective parents look like? Pastors work with effective
moms and dads every day. I asked nearly a hundred pastors randomly chosen from among the
best I know, to nominate effective parents. They
sent me hundreds of names. I then wrote each of
the nominated families (three times before I was
done) asking them to share with me how effective
parents do their effective parenting. I discovered
a lot.

First, almost all were surprised anyone had
noticed them—or thought they were effective.
That surprise became an effective parenting

"given." Second, without exception, effective moms and dads tussled with that word *effective*. Even if—just maybe—their families might qualify for that "e-word," it hardly fit *them*. That kind of resistance showed up so consistently that it became an unfailing characteristic of effective parents.

A third thing I noticed was that effective parents were not alone in their effectiveness. They were invariably surrounded by (or surrounded themselves with): effective grandparents, effective friends and neighbors, effective brothers and sisters, effective relatives. I finally concluded they must have effective cats, dogs, and parakeets too. Effectiveness attracts effectiveness.

But, even after all my listening, reading, and checking, I still wasn't satisfied that everyone who needed a hearing had been brought into our learning loop, especially since this specific book has the twin concern of (1) effective parenting and (2) how effective parenting is practiced in rearing children four years of age and younger. How will those younger parents—effective parents in training—get a hearing?

To gain their inclusion I sent a questionnaire to the parent/parents of every fourth child that was born in our parish over the past three years. That was 90 or so questionnaires—a large cross section by statistical standards. I read the responses. They came in fast. Guess what? After the fifteenth response, little surfaced that was new. All young parents were facing almost identical concerns.

In the light of that, I sent no more question-naires to the families of our parish. Instead, I took these same questions to young couples across the nation, and I interviewed dozens as I traveled. The results? Can you guess? The stories they told me differed a little, but the theme of the stories was constant. I concluded that there are identifiable, even predictable, views and insights held by effec-tive parents—even among parental novices. They are in this book.

Finally, I worried about some of those who were nominated by pastors but had not responded. So I phoned a few, asking them to help me inter-pret their silence. Two answers surfaced. (1) Many hadn't gotten around to it—yet. I received one let-ter a year after my last due date! (2) Most of the silent ones didn't feel they communicated well through the written word. But talk? Did they ever! Then the fun began.

I sorted the 1,000–plus pages of letters, notes, memos, and clippings I had gathered, looking for common threads. They surfaced quickly and easily. About 14 categories held up across the age levels, across all family sizes and age spreads, across the various sociological and geographical locations. There was no essential difference in the response of a doctor or dock worker (I had both), the rich or those struggling to make ends meet (ditto), Tex-ans or Virginians (or Kansans, Minnesotans, Cali-fornians—with a dozen other states heard from too). Some themes were stronger at one family age level than at others, but all the threads showed up in some form at every level, whether the children in the family were newborn or nearly adult.

Oh, yes: names and locations. I scrambled both in the book. Their accurate inclusion made no difference to the results. I did, however, use authentic names and locations. All the names and places are real to some piece of the quoted material. If any contributors want to try identifying themselves, they are welcome to try, with this caution: Similar stories came in from many different parts of the country; I doubt you can find yours—at least not for sure.

So let's be at it. Let's listen to effective parents, old and young. It's their book. The chapter subjects are of their choosing. I organized them for ease of presentation, but I have not prioritized or ranked them. Each chapter segment is but one powerful part of the whole.

So, here's to effective parents! Especially, here's to effective parents of the youngest of God's special people as they move from being babies to toddlers! God loves all moms and dads. Maybe that's why one of our favorite names for Him is *Father.*

Mighty Rivers Meet, and Mesh?

---◆---

I am inspired by my parents' faith. Every day.

—An Oregon Mother

Thousands of miles from the Atlantic Ocean, deep within the Brazilian rain forests, two gargantuan rivers collide. From due west, tumbling out of the Peruvian Andes, the Amazon, already a mile wide, rushes to the meeting. The Columbian highlands to the northwest produce a second river, the Rio Negra. At a powerful, but more ponderous rate, it lumbers through dark wetlands to its destiny.

And then it happens. Near Manaus those mighty rivers smash into each other. With a roar and a roiling of the waters, they try elbowing each other aside, struggling to fit into one river bed. But they do not mingle immediately. The chalky brown of the Amazon maintains itself, separated from the deeper bronze of the Rio Negra. One hugs the near bank, the other the far one, for nearly 20 miles—still two rivers. Only after miles of pushing along side by side do their differences slowly soften and finally blend. The two become one. In their final uniting they are much more than either had been before. A thousand miles upstream from the Atlantic Ocean those combined rivers are wide enough, and deep enough, to give ocean liners passage. And they have one name: Amazon.

Does that opening descriptive sound familiar? Have you seen something like that? I say yes. While few who read this book may ever view these great rivers struggling to become one, everyone has seen a life event similar to this mighty melding. Where? At a wedding.

In a wedding, two pasts, each as powerful as either Brazilian river, meet and, with disguised intensity, begin a blending process. There, in a subdued moment, with the church quiet, a beautifully attired bridal party in attendance, and their parents beaming approval from the front rows, two enormous and churning pasts come hurtling at each other in the persons of the delicate bride and her handsome groom. As the pastor announces the nuptials, the two combine, like the Amazon and the Rio Negra, claiming one name and occupying one bed—but not without a struggle. Though the two key participants walk out of the church claiming one name, there's more to it.

For starters, fragments of their separate and mysterious yesterdays must be recognized and tagged. Distinct memories, enough to fill a library, have to be shared—and explained. Two family histories need telling and receptive understanding. Intricate family traditions must unravel. How long will all that take? The 50 minutes of the service? More like 50 years.

Some elements of a couple's separate yesterdays will never fully mingle, even though intense and intentional efforts at mixing go on and on. Want to hear what all that inter-family churning can sound like?

Why do I pick today on this dreary rainy morning to write you? My brother of 45 years died last night and went to His Savior. I am reflecting on how he, my two other brothers, my sister, and I were raised. My parents influenced not only the five of us but the raising of my five children as well.

Those sentences are a blip, a glimpse, a flash of remembering from one grandmother's past. In them, across all the years, the living hands of her long-dead parents are acknowledged as still affecting her—and her children. It's a three-generation impact. And how many more succeeding generations will feel her parents' touch? Who knows? Add this: Powerful as her story is, it's only *half* of the whole. Her husband brings an entirely different "yesterday" into this equation as well.

Family roots, family history, the family of origin—call it what you will—was a recurring theme in the letters and comments of effective parents.

News? Not really. Social scientists exploring diverse cultures have long reported on the power in our past. It's not debatable. But it's often under-estimated and unacknowledged. "Look out," say effective parents. Pay attention to your individual and coupled yesterdays.

Listen to some young parents in their twenties as they reflect this theme:

- *I end up saying and doing a lot of the same things my parents did. I also intentionally do some things different, such as telling Kurt "I love you" and hugging and kissing a lot. Those were things that my parents didn't do—and I wish they had.*

- *My parenting skills are a repeat of my parents', whether for good or bad. But I can still choose which to change, modify, or repeat. I think the deepest moral values I have definitely stem from my origins. But at the same time, there are several things in our growing that both my husband and I remember as detrimental. We discuss these things and make an effort not to go those routes.*

- *Our yesterday affects us in two ways. On the one hand, we don't do certain things that were done to us, but we remember certain other precious memories that we want to create again. What our parents did is our only experience with parent-*

ing—we have to pull ideas from some-where. That's why we believe that parents raise their own children the way they were raised.

- *With the decline of the extended family, most kids are only exposed to one example of parenting style: that of their own parents. When it comes time to raise our kids, that's the only experience we have to draw on. Isn't that why dysfunctional parenting is passed from generation to generation? Fortunately, good parenting is too.*

- *Radically different families of origin can be a source of conflict between parents. I tend to be more calm and easy-going about our child's behavior than my wife. This can be a problem, especially when the children's behavior is driving my wife nuts.*

As I reflect on the pros and cons that all the groups told me about, I realize their message is real. I am a product of my past. My families of origin (Muellers on one side, Steinkamps on the other, with shadowy antecedent groups stretching back into history) affect what I eat on Christmas Eve—what else but oyster stew—and how I dress for church—save a white shirt for Sunday—and how I handle finances—don't borrow for a "want," only for a need. The way we hide Easter eggs—Audrey's history is preeminent in this area, when Christmas gifts are opened in our house, and the proper method for trimming the grass along the front walk all come storming out of our yesterdays with as much power as any Brazilian rain-forest river. To this day I carry a pocket knife, just like my dad taught me to: You never know when you're going to need a sturdy blade.

The many effective families who surfaced this concern had ways of talking about their durable yesterdays. One wrote:

> *My dad has been gone 11 years now. But I daily remember something from his life. He was a Standard Oil agent in Sheboygan. The winters were brutal and his job was keeping people warm by keeping their fuel tanks full. Sometimes the phone would ring in the middle of the night—a customer was out of fuel. Dad would get out of bed, put on his heaviest clothes, and drive to the bulk plant. There he would load a truck in the bitter cold and drive to the customer's house to deliver fuel. There was no extra charge. This was his service. He just wanted to take care of his customers. Now that's Christian living.*

Reading those words, can you imagine all the times and all the ways that one incident has affected him? Will his wife ever really understand her husband's drive to do some things in a certain way—just like his dad did—without the same memory bank?

His story is no exception. Here are four more. Think of each as a mighty cascade of yesterday spilling out of the dimmer reaches of someone's past. All still have power and impact.

- *My dad always liked sports. I grew up with some knowledge of sports. Little did I realize the advantage this would give me in life. My husband played three sports in high school and two in college. From the time they were born, our children spent hours in their father's arms (later in his lap or crawling all over him) as he watched a sporting event. To this day we all talk about sports. Our daughter's husband was surprised at her sport knowledge.*

Her father's love of sports became a life-changing, cross-generational force of consequence for this woman. When her husband came courting, do you think he had any idea the advantage his love of sports gave him? That advantage was a gift from a father-in-law he did not yet know. It played a part in the life of the next generation too. We better pay attention to what we teach our children to like.

- *Dad was transferred my senior year in high school. He delayed the family move for a year until I graduated. During that time he was only home on weekends and spent the week living in a hotel. I am ashamed to admit how little I understood or appreciated the sacrifice he and Mom made for me. I was too wrapped up in myself to consider how difficult the separation must have been. Now I'm amazed.*

Now the questions: Do you think her parents did what they did to teach her a lesson? Or was their sacrifice motivated by a love for their child and an unwillingness to uproot her at a critical point in her life? No matter what we think, she's already claimed a conclusion that will affect her as long as she lives. As she shares it with her children, the next generation is affected too.

- *My father was an enormous help during the time of separation between my husband and me. He was actually a surrogate dad and he helped me through the pregnancy and the birth of my third child. Many days he would say to me, "This, too, shall pass." That saying brought me some comfort. But the example of his strong faith brought me more. It is much easier to understand the concept of a loving heavenly Father when you have a loving earthly father.*

The rest of this inspirational letter breathes with the spirit of Christ as it was lived out by her dad. There's no question in my mind that his great grandchildren, in some tomorrow, will respond to a crisis in their life in unconscious imitation of a dimly recalled great grandfather. In establishing powerful standards, families of origin set great forces in motion.

- *When I was a child, it was a fact of life that our family attended church regularly even though my three brothers and I gave our folks some static when we were in our teens and college years. When we lived at home, everyone went to church. We still do. In addition to regular church attendance, my parents set a good example of regular contributions. My dad would say, "You can never outgive God."*

Later in her letter this lady mentioned she never misses church today. Any idea why?

So what's the point for our younger parents? The point is simple: A lifelong love of athletics can be started by how a mother/father plays ball with a child; a love of learning grows as little ones see parents handle books and deeper subjects; honesty is infectious down the generations. The mighty Amazon or the Rio Negra begin somewhere as a trickle. The past has power. In the world of your children you are a part of the past, and your handling of them will be the memory out of which they make decisions.

Stories from people's past are not all positive. There is darkness in yesterday too. Some of it is so awesomely dark that only the finest professional assistance can bring relief. Yet, in the hands of effective parents, yesterday's bad can be turned to good. One couple mixed their separate negative rememberings, giving them a new spin:

There was a lot of discord in Bryan's family during his childhood. Though my life was somewhat more stable, my dad had a bad temper that flared often. Neither of us wanted to live in that kind of environment again. We talked during our courtship about our home being peaceful and loving, without yelling and screaming. It is.

A Nebraska dad recalls some of his darker yesterdays and then shows why he is an effective parent today:

My growing-up years were difficult for me. I was always compared with my brother. I now believe I was verbally abused. I don't communicate with my brother these days. The last visit with my parents was a hard visit, as I was again confronted by my parents as to something they accused me of doing. How I was treated, and still am, affects the way I treat our boys. We love both boys. I am trying hard to not abuse them verbally. I try desperately not to compare them. I know those feelings.

But what's the real point to all this? Is it only to show that we are all somehow products of our past?

I'll let an Arkansas father answer that question. He states:

Our sons are four, six, and seven. We are raising our teenagers right now.

Four, six, seven—he realizes he can't change yesterday. Whatever yesterday was, it is beyond his reach. It affects him. Locked in time he cannot affect it. But he can affect tomorrow. Today is tomorrow's yesterday.

While no one can change yesterday, we do influence every today before it becomes a "yesterday." The wit to see the truth in that, and the will to do something about it, is one characteristic of effective parents. If, as they do so, they are blessed by memories of their own effective parents and how those parents treated them in the past, today's effective mom and dad have a great advantage.

Just so you don't think I'm on a philosophical binge, check the following letters and decode their message about the hookup between yesterday and tomorrow.

From Minnesota: *My love for God came through my parents, both immigrants. And of my parents, most of it came from my mother. My parents lived their lives with God at the head. They have both gone to heaven. But as I look back with fondness on my childhood, I see how they let the Lord lead their lives. I am teaching my children what I learned.*

And two from Kansas:

My parents are my role models. They are the most intuitive, generous, and kind Christian people that I know. Our home life was great. It wasn't always perfect, but there was plenty of love, encouragement, and stability.

I give all credit to God for putting me in my family. Beside being God-fearing and forgiving parents, my mother and father instilled a sense of service in me that I feel has been part of my lifelong walk with God.

From New York too: *As a fairly young, new mother I am operating on common sense and emulating the family in which I grew.*

Traditions, history, and memories are what each of us brings to our marriage. A husband's positive river of yesterday, combined with a similar stream from his spouse, equips effective parents. Then they, in turn, influence their children's future as they build with them memories of how life is best lived today. It's a wise mom or dad who truly understands they have little control over their children, and such that they have is short-lived and minimally effective. But the influence of memory—what a force! Tomorrow's remembering is under our control today. Baby-carriage parents, especially, can shape what is coming by some things they can do right now.

- *Talk about the past with your partner. Intentionally lift up and discuss the insight that it is the combination of your pasts that your children deal with. Identify some stories from yesterday your children need to hear and understand.*

- *As each parent talks about yesterdays, give room to tell the whole story. Let each partner listen and ask questions. You will discover new and important things about each other's past.*

- *While there is still time, interview both sets of grandparents on video or audiotape. Talk to them one by one. Ask about all the relatives either can recall, their earliest memories, what it was like to be raised where they were, their family life. When I did this with my nearly 80-year-old parents, my mother said, after hearing a comment by Dad, "You never told me that!" His response: "You never asked."*

- *Start a family scrapbook. Get your parents to identify people and places in old photos.*

- *Make a family tree. Nothing complicated. List the people, including the little ones of today. Show them that they have a place and that their names are important.*

- *Finish the sentence, "One thing Mom/ Dad taught me that I want our baby to grow up knowing is ...." Then put that sentence into play. Explain your sentence so your partner can support your goal. As the children grow, involve them in your goals too.*

What gives a family hope it can survive the mixing of two great forces of history? Check the next chapter. Meanwhile, remember your roots and their power.

First Comes Love

---◆---

The prime ingredient in a marriage that works is the husband and wife's love for one another. That takes time, work, and prayer. When we were dating, we did not use the word love. We agreed that the words "I love you" should be reserved for the real thing. When finally I felt that God had answered my prayers and that Janie was the one, I told her I loved her for the first time. It took her a while longer.

—A Texas Husband

Our children know for a fact that we love them very much, and we show it as often as possible with words and action.

—A Missouri Mom

I remember watching little girls at play under a calendar-perfect oak tree. The afternoon sun, slipping toward evening, dappled them in a soft autumn blend of creamy light. Two twirled the rope at a steady pace while the third danced in and above its dangerous entanglements with practiced ease. All sing-songed: "FIRST comes love/ and THEN comes marriage/ and THEN comes the BA-by/ in the BA-by carriage .... " Will that agile little girl with such endless energy never slip or slow down?

Separated from that memory by time and distance, I find myself wondering, "Who was the brilliant teacher/moralist/poet of yesterday who composed their simple rap?" Those little ladies, looking to be not yet 10, knew the proven path to effective parenting, even putting each step in order: (1) love, (2) marriage, (3) the baby. In that sequence the baby is most likely to arrive wanted and protected, never left as a loved, but still heavy, load for one parent. Two caring adults, practiced toward each other in the art of caring and loving intimacy, are what's best for all when the baby arrives.

That progressive chant is sometimes twisted in life. Maybe it's the love that comes under attack. In the cruel brightness of the morning many a trusting victim has realized that what was portrayed last night as changeless love was more likely ordinary lust. 2 Samuel 13 reports a story of loveless love wrapping it up with the classic synopsis of post-passion pain, "[He] hated her with intense hatred. In fact, he hated her more than he had loved her" (v. 15).

But lust doesn't only turn into hate. Disdain, disinterest, and disregard are other possibilities. It can become a baby, too, who enters the world with a single mom. No happy rope-jumping rhyme brightens that scenario! Why? It's backward. Incomplete. Inverted.

God's intention in His love/marriage/baby cycle (and it is His) is that love comes first and then sticks around for a lifetime. Effective parents agree with God on the place and power of love. An Iowa husband wants the world to know:

> *We feel that love and respect for each other is pivotal to peace in the home. In Scripture, husbands are told to love their wives and wives are told to respect their husbands. Through little effort on our part God has brought this about in our marriage. It is pure grace and we know it. We love each other and are satisfied in the relationship we enjoy. We are not exceptional people. Our gifts, abilities, and talents fall into the average range and if we were to describe ourselves, it would be "ordinary."*

Lest any are taken in by their use of the word *ordinary*, they are understating things. Their family opened its home to dozens of rejected community kids over the years—even adopted many. It just goes to show: What is amazing to many is little more than ordinary to lovers.

I delight in love. Such a word! And yet, would you believe that it is nowhere defined? Not in the Bible. Not in the dictionary. It is not defined. It *is* described. Even 1 Corinthians 13, the greatest love chapter of Scripture, does not define love. It describes how love acts. Love is kind, gentle, doesn't insist on its own way, lasts forever, and so much more.

That indefinable character of love is why countless songs have been written about love, with more to come. Every new life experience, each new invention, all human adventures, carry the potential for being a newer description of love. But, no matter. Whether love is definable or not, effective families and effective parents know what it looks like and how it feels. They think it is great. The jump-rope girls are right in the rhyme, "First comes love."

Do you recall the theme of the last chapter? Most parents say they first experienced love in their homes. One reports:

There was always love in my home as a child. My parents were from different religious backgrounds and different ethnic backgrounds, but there was love.

I'll let five other comments represent the range and the intensity of how effective parents feel on the subject. The comments come from the four corners of the country—and mid-America too.

- North: *Love is the most important ingredient of life—God's and the parents'. We have always felt the Lord's presence in our lives. He doesn't promise us a smooth life. He does promise He will always be* with us. He loves us, and His love allows us to surmount the lows and revel in the highs.

- East: *I not only love Nora as my wife but also as my closest friend. I think that has impacted our kids. We have our share of problems and roadblocks and we have not been perfect parents who made no mistakes. But we know well that we are perfect in the blood of Jesus and can go on because He loves, understands, and forgives us.*

- South: *It's a risky business describing what makes for effective parenting. Just as the people in the Old Testament misinterpreted God's desire for a relationship with them into a list of dos and don'ts for a righteous life, so many parents could read your book as a cookbook, hoping to stamp out "good Christian kids" like so many cutout cookies. This may be a desire motivated by a real love for their kids because the world is full of real dangers. But raising kids is far too complex a process, one really beyond understanding, to reduce it to a set of procedures which, when carried out, will produce healthy kids. The topic of Christian parenting must be discussed in the context of the mystery of the love of God. Why would anyone want to offer their posses-*

sions, their time, their youth, their very selves to prepare someone they love to leave one day. The fact that many parents, Christian and non-Christian alike, do this testifies to the fact that we are created for a high purpose: love.

- West: *I'm sure God can work in a relationship where there is only one parent, if that parent is committed to the Lord's leading. But in our family there are two of us. We both have a central focus that is Jesus Christ. The extreme love that Jesus had for us made it possible for us to come together as one and stay together.*

- Central: *Our faith in God has always been at the core of our relationship. The inscription in our wedding bands is "God loves us." I guess you could say that is our family motto. If we don't have to worry about who we are because we know whose we are, that is very freeing.*

Our effective parents wrote about the love they first knew in their families of origin. They wrote beautifully about the love they experience now. I have love letters written by them that elevate the art of expressing affection by husbands and wives for each other to new heights. Listen:

I love my husband so much. Our love and understanding of each other has grown

*through many trials. But sometimes I just
don't like him. About the time I start to feel
like that I remind myself of all my faults that
he has put up with. That makes me realize
how thankful I should be to have his love
and know it's mine without a doubt.*

Tell me. Is she in love? Oh my!

A husband pens this love letter about his partner:

*All our lives Eileen has been the one that
kept us pointed in the right direction—
toward the cross. We've had our share of the
"shaky" moments; all families do. What I'm
trying to say is that Eileen has played a very
important role in making us effective, if
there is such a descriptive term for parents
and family. The Beach Boys once recorded a
song called, "God Only Knows What I'd Be
without You." I've often wondered what I'd
be without Eileen. If I could have one wish
for our son as he goes out on his own, that
wish would be that he would meet someone
as caring as his mother.*

Another, from a lady who has been very sick.
Telling about her husband she says:

*We have grown in closeness, and my trust
of him reaches to the sky. I know a wonderful truth—John will always love me. After
all, he loved me when I was **bald!** He loved
me when I was sick, unreasonable, and mis-*

*erable. I feel an incredible security with him
and a great admiration. If love heals cancer,
I'm healed.*

A last one, the content of which was often repeated but seldom as eloquently. Written by a wife about her husband, the same thoughts were expressed by many husbands about their wives:

We recently celebrated our tenth anniversary. We are still very much in love and committed to each other without reservation. Our marriage is more stressed than in the early years because of our three small boys. I now understand the surveys showing how the unhappiest years of marriage are when the children are at home. But I could not ask for a better mate. He is a constant and strong presence, always giving me strength. He tries to live as a Christian father and as the husband presented in the Bible as head of the household, setting an example for the boys in their Christian education—loving and faithful.

But how do you get that kind of love and then keep it alive in a marriage and a family? Effective parents are very practical on this subject. They do things for each other as expressions of their affection. They stated, again and again, that love is enhanced by parental cooperation and care. Like taking turns bedding the children down for the night. Or one baby-sits, alone, just so that the other gets a chance to be out of the house without kids tagging along. Some reported showing love by dropping important (to them) outside interests that were making their partner's life more difficult. One husband wrote this litany of love:

When something needs to be done, I just do it. I used to expect my wife to clean the house and do the laundry during the day since she was already home running her day-care center for five or six kids. I never really said much about it. I just dropped hints, and every once in a while, she would surprise me by getting everything in order. I later had the opportunity to fill in for her. Now I know the truth. I don't know how she keeps track of all those kids, let alone gets anything else done. I also realized that if she had a job outside the home, the work would have to be done by both in the evenings and on weekends. So I don't say anything any more. I do what I can to help.

Cooperation and care are important, but the flood of comment came on one subject: spending time with each other. Alone.

First, they make sure there is daily time with each other alone at home.

After God, Charlie and I are number one in each other's lives and the girls know it. We spend time with each other every night after the children are in bed.

Another? *While you have to realize that when you are a family, you give up some of what you once had, you still need to have special time with your wife or husband. You can't always be mom and dad.*

One more? *Be sure to spend some time every night with your mate. If you don't invest time in that relationship, your family will reflect it.*

Not everyone was openly on that bandwagon. One husband came at it backward—and repentant:

I should spend more time with my wife, alone. We are together a lot as family, but the two of us rarely get away. We tend to argue a lot about many things. Sometimes I think we are too involved (is that possible?) with our kids and not involved enough with each other.

His four sentences need to be studied as a unit. Effective parents would say there is a cause-and-effect relationship at work within them. And who's the cause?

There's more to being with each other than carving out minutes and hours at home. Our effective parents are wiser than that. They make sure they get away together, for longer periods, at least once a year.

From Texas: *Roger and I try to get away at least once a year. Long ago we decided this was important to our relationship. We try to forget all our problems and any crisis at home and concentrate on each other.*

An Ohio couple put it this way: *It's important for us to take time to be with each other, whether it is to walk around the block, have an evening out, or take three or four days away. This time is used to talk and listen to each other, to set goals for our family, review the past, and build up and encourage each other.*

Love needs time. Later in this book effective parents say a lot more about time as a separate subject. Right now time is important as it relates to love—and effective parenting.

Many effective parents have a proportioned and genuine appreciation of themselves. It is scientifically verifiable that our respect for others grows proportionately to the respect we have for ourselves. Of course! What is that but a reflection of Jesus' words in Matt. 19:19, repeated in so many other places in the Bible, "You shall love your neighbor as yourself?" Effective parents believe it.

One wrote: *Our marriage is based on trust. We are honest with each other and try to communicate effectively. We have different views but we agree on basics. There are things we accept about each other that may be irritants but are overlooked because they are unimportant. I tend to be more emo-*

tional and Tom is more analytical. He teasingly calls me a "soft scientist" which is supposed to make me see things his way. But it never does.

Does that lady have self-respect? And love? No question.

And this: *My husband: what a man! Dependable, tolerant, gentle, a godly man, my friend. He always allows me to develop me. He respects me and my opinions.*

Her husband encourages that self-respect. In so doing he shows he knows how important it is. His caring doesn't quench the fires of love—it pours gasoline on them.

A solid and proper love of self affects the children of effective parents too. One daughter, a teen writing from college, ends a three-page eulogy to her parents by telling how their rearing shaped her outlook on life. She says:

I have a strong sense of myself. I like me and the person my parents showed me how to become. Where I struggle is knowing whether others like me ... but not enough to change in order to be loved by the masses.

And then she wrote another three pages praising her parents.

Years ago a California teenager gave me a sentence to share with others who are pressured to do what they feel is wrong. When she is asked to do something that her sensitized Christian conscience tells her is not right, she says, "I can't do that—it wouldn't be right for me." With those 10 words she claims the high ground of human love: a genuine and biblical love of self that motivates and frees her to love others.

Interviews with newer mothers and fathers turn up the same insights. The reports about the importance of love coming from the different age groups doesn't vary. Young mother Betty says:

Love between parents is terribly important. Without a solid, loving relationship I can't imagine how a couple could survive the first difficult, stressful, sleepless weeks and months of parenthood. Later on, I know that love between the parents is infectious. When Andy and I hug, Suzanne runs right over to get into the act.

See how insightful new parents can be?

Do our effective parents of every age have anything to say about how we might teach this love? Yes. In a way.

It sort of happens by the grace of God, writes a Colorado mother. *You do your best to teach your children as you have been taught, to love one another. And when a husband and wife love each other—perhaps that's it—the love spills over to each family member, just like it was spilled over on us.*

My children are precious to me and I love them all. But God gave me their father first and I have loved him longest. Our children are building families of their own while we are growing older together. In love.

For those who aren't sure about the importance of love, let me share this from the daughter of effective New Mexico parents:

As long as I can remember, I have been told that I am loved, special, and cherished. I know that no matter how low I fall, my parents—like the prodigal's father—will welcome me back with open arms. We are a very touchy-feely family.

Effective parents stir up love. They don't just wait for love to happen. They do loving things, until—lo, and behold—there it is!

In specific? Here are five to-dos from younger parents, all supported and reinforced by their seniors.

- *Practice the saying of the words. Say them: "I love you." Say them in the morning. Say them in private. Say them on the street. Say them in front of the children. Let them hear the words that present the feelings of love for one another.*

- *Back the words with the acts of love. Hugging and kissing. Yes! But the tender sensitivities of love need to be shown too: the little courtesies, the kind remarks, the sweet gentilities. Often young parents have limited budgets. None of these things cost a cent.*

- *Together let parents both say and do love with their children. Explain the mysterious ways of love, not just when you are doing something that seems to contradict love ("I'm only taking away your toy because I love you") but also when it seems so natural and obvious. Develop special things: special plates, special foods, special places, special attentions. Explain them all as ways of saying and doing love.*

- *Surround children with symbols of Another's love: a cross in their room, a religious plaque, a picture, a poem. Let them know that your love is but an extension of His love. Immerse them in the wonder of affection both human and divine.*

- *Look around at others who love their children. Don't imitate their cruder expressions of love that overwhelm children with* **things.** *But imitate those loving touches that you find hidden everywhere—any number in the pages of this book. Adopt the best. Adapt the rest.*

Finally, let's get set for one of love's most common testing grounds: change. Times change. Children change. Choices change. Change happens so often and develops such an apprehension in people that it's almost as if it is the enemy of the family, a burden to caring parents, and the contradiction of love. What do you think?

Tempore Mutantur...
and How!

"We have three terrific but challenging children: Lonnie, 12, middle school and hormones (yuk!); Angela, 9, beautiful and temperamental; Nickie, 3½, the bruiser.
—A Mississippi Mother

The more I live the more I am aware that tough times are not unique to us. It's part of life and who we are.
—An Illinois Father

When the kids were little, my mother told me I read too many books about child development and such. I disagreed and still do. It's important to read about child development and what to expect at certain ages. That doesn't mean that everything I read or hear is right, but I'm open to suggestions.
—An Iowa Single Parent

More years ago than now seem possible, I was a sophomore in high school trying to learn Latin.

The grammar/vocabulary approach was tough and I was getting nowhere. One day I came upon a book of translated Latin quotations. I memorized them. In the process I picked up enough vocabulary and grammar to pass the course. In addition, I developed a lifelong love of language, Latin included.

One of those Latin sayings I memorized was *Tempore mutantur et nos mutamur in illes.* Translated it means "The times are changing and we are changing in them." Two profound insights, 2,000 years old. Insight 1: Times keep changing. Insight 2: So do we.

Until 150 years ago educators were not convinced life changes were so abundant, so inevitable, or so consequential. The major changes in life were few—two to be exact. First came childhood and youth. Then came adulthood and old age. The change took place somewhere between nine and 11 years of age. Eleven-year-olds could be midshipmen in the British Navy, with command and responsibility. Nine-year-olds worked and died in factories and mines, victims of long hours and cruel expectations. Childhood was brief.

But *tempore mutantur*—times changed. Our idea of life's stages is more sophisticated. Childhood is not one unit of life. It is segmented too. We further divide the teen years into three, or more, portions. Paralleling the teen divisions, old age also is divided. Now the normally acknowledged number of times of change in life are many more. We even developed stages of prebirth, our time in the womb. By eight weeks the fetus' heart is beating and has been doing so for a month. Change. In the fourth month its hands grasp and its feet kick. Change. At seven months the fetus responds to sound and can perceive light. Change. By its birth day the newborn can distinguish patterns, movement, light, and color. Change.

Change, which starts long before birth, continues and intensifies. By three months most babies can laugh. Six months? He/she will yank at your hair with such zest your eyes will tear. Many (not all) seven-month-olds can say "Mama." At 12 months most can climb stairs. All that is change—for the baby, for parents, for everyone. One growth chart I use divides life into 11 major change stages, the first three taking place before the child is 10 years of age. To illustrate the speed and sweep of change in the child that every new mother and dad deal with daily, let's just peek at major elements of Stage 1 and Stage 2.

The first 18 months comprise the greatest period of growth in all of life! *All* of life. Children grow wonderfully from birth to age 1 and then double in size between their first and second birthdays. Change? Baby's first (and favorite) words are "Dada," "Mama," "mine," and "no." His or her interest span starts from a few seconds and peaks out at a minute or so—for some things. Large muscles are developing in Stage 1. That means accidents—and understandable awkwardness—that

can be perceived as aggressiveness or lack of atten-
tiveness. It's neither. Just change.

Sometime within Stage 2 (ages 3–5), many
children will invent an imaginary (but very real to
them) playmate. They become self-critical, saying
things like "Me a good (or bad) boy." They start
talking incessantly, pressing constantly for attention, usually by calling out your name over and
over and over and over. Familiar? Their interest
spans expand making TV and some activities very
compelling. They show hand preference and begin
small muscle development that makes it possible to
color in the lines and put smaller puzzles together.
Each change is an enormous event in childhood.
Each signals change.

I won't continue cataloging changes in the
child for a couple of reasons: (1) There are a lot of
excellent books on the subject of childhood stages
and change; (2) The focus of this book is not the
child but the parent. Notwithstanding, this whirl-
wind tour through Stages 1 and 2 offers an effective lesson in parenting, especially for those who
are just beginning: Change is a part of life and
never changes! That insight is Parenting 101 first-
day data. A young father who just "enrolled" wrote:

*Just two days after our daughter was born
we brought her home. I was on cloud 9.
After being in the delivery room, I felt she
was such a miracle! However it seemed to
turn into a nightmare. She wouldn't go to
sleep. At 2 a.m. the first night she was home,*

I was lying on my back, staring at the ceiling, listening to her cry and wondering if this was going to be worth it. Well, it sure has been!

C-H-A-N-G-E. Six letters. Such an innocent looking, but persistent, little word. It keeps coming back all life long. You change. People around you change. Circumstances change. Community values change. Choices change. Those old Romans were right: *Tempore mutantur*—Times are changing! They compounded their correctness with that addition, " ... and we are changing in them." Effective parents recognize that reality. Do you?

Test your change perception by identifying two big changes that have happened since you were married. Write them down. And now do the same for your partner—name two major ways he or she has changed. Talk with your partner about both. Ask your partner to pick the big changes from his or her perspective.

Then, together, note two changes in your life circumstance that make both of you react in a different way. Finally, focus on your children. What have been their two major changes in the last year?

You are well on your way to parental effectiveness if you can discuss those four aspects of change. Note where you have handled change well and where you haven't done so well. Claim the right to a second chance. Effective parents do that. In the doing they raise the level of their effectiveness. But how? How, specifically, do effective parents become experts?

A Delaware mother, an effective parent, the child of effective parents, gives us one clue when she writes:

Today, in my own family, the names and faces and personalities are different when compared to the family in which I was raised. So there isn't just one blueprint that will work. Times change. Problems change. Circumstances change. But there is One **who does not change:** *Our God, our help in ages past and our hope for years to come. He will continue to walk with our families until He makes us part of His one eternal family some day.*

She has carved out an expert's approach to change by noting the One who transcends change. Then she clings to Him.

Another—this time a Kansas mother—adds understanding of how it works in real life families:

Babies learn at birth about dependence. That knowledge and sense never really changes. It diminishes as the kids grow up when they come to learn that Mom and Dad will be with them through thick and thin as they grow up. But children should be raised to know they will eventually find someone to love, leave their parents, and cleave to their spouse as God commanded and do so with the almost contradictory knowledge that even though they are then independent and self-sustaining, they will always be able to depend upon their family.

How's that for a resumé of the place and importance of change and an understanding of how it gets applied in daily life?

I'm not exactly sure how to word this, writes a New York father, *but some people say parenting is the only job for which there are no classes or instruction. I don't think a class would help because parenting and "family-ing" involves personality and the changing interactions of those personalities. One method that may work with one child will not necessarily work with another. We have found that what works one day doesn't always work the next day—with the same child.*

This dad has come to peace with change, accepting unpredictability in change as a key element. To put it simply: Different children change in different ways at different times.

Another attaches learning-how-to-deal-with-change to a specific preparental experience:

Two difficult events which, in our opinion, strengthened our marriage happened in 1989 and 1991: miscarriages. We knew that they were not the will of God. We knew they were not a result of our inadequacies as par-

ents. We knew they were signs and results of an imperfect world. We put our trust in Him as a loving and just God who works for good in the people He calls His own. God strengthened us through these times. We now have a greater appreciation for our children and the other gifts God has given.

So how do effective parents develop expertise in dealing with change? Quotes suggest *that parents trust in God's presence through the best and worst, recognizing that change has a value— and an unpredictability—even in the face of awesome life experiences.* That sentence needs to be thoughtfully honed to conform comfortably to your life experiences. Do that as you hear more about change from effective parents. Match their experiences and understanding to yours.

More about change: It can happen quick as a wink or slow as a stare. When our four children were small, my wife was depressingly sure that each, in turn, would waddle off to first grade diapered, a "guilty" draped over the shoulder, a thumb in mouth, carrying a nippled bottle. More out of love than understanding, I assured her that would never happen. But a young mother struggling with the slowness of some change did not find my brave assurances very reassuring.

What Audrey and I needed was a broader picture that more fully recognized the pace, place, and process of change. We could have used the advice of an Illinois mother who sees change from a better perspective than ours and who adapted her effective parenting to it:

When our children were little, I played "little" games. As they grew older and their interests changed, I tried to stay tuned to what was important to them. We spent a lot of time together, but I was careful to be a mother and not become a pal. I found their strengths and encouraged each to develop them.

She understood the inevitability of change and got out in front of it so she could be there while it was happening. In the process she even shaped it a bit.

For a study of even more complex change, visit effective parents in a blending family. A Washington twosome writes:

Over the past three years we have seen lots of changes. In the beginning it was his family and my family doing things together. We are now getting to the point where we begin thinking of "our family." We have had enough experiences together to give us some sense of history. We can now say, "Remember when ... " and it will be about something we experienced as a family unit. With the passage of time and God's direction, this bond will become stronger. At first Bob and I wanted this sense of family to happen immediately. It has taken longer than we would like. However, we have learned to focus on what we as a family have accomplished rather than what is still left to do.

That quote summarizes almost all we have presented to this point and contains a useful collection of what needs to be known about change: (1) It's fast most of the time but awesomely slow at others, (2) It is usually unpredictable, (3) God is at work in it, (4) We need to interpret it—correctly. Those are four key insights into the nature of change.

But how, specifically, do effective parents not only face change but deal with it? What skill or skills are needed? Let me lift up a few.

Breathing within the interviews are two skills so deceptively simple that they can be missed easily. Yet if a parent is to make change an ally and a friend, both skills must be understood and practiced. One is **negotiating**. The other is **renegotiating**.

I was first flagged on these family skills by one of the Christian family's best friends, Dr. Donald R. Bardill of Florida State University. He describes these twins as helping families develop rules, and then create the rules on rules.

It starts like this: All families have and need rules. Even the least effective families have them though they may be intentionally ambiguous. (We'll let our effective families deal with that problem in their chapter on communication.) But back to rules.

While all families have rules, most don't have rules on rules—that is, how rules are changed. They do not have a way to intentionally deal with outmoded, ineffective, or inappropriate rules. When rules need changing, and everyone knows it, the family just starts doing things differently instead of having an intentional and reasoned way to change. In that process there is a lot of fighting and misunderstanding and hurt feelings. None of those things build family.

Effective families are different. They first make rules for talking together about issues that deal with change. In effective families, parents make efforts to explain (even to the youngest) why it's important to do things a certain way. The process of setting rules via discussion and explanation is what negotiating is all about. Negotiating does not mean the family votes on everything. It may, but that's not the point. Effective families work at everyone understanding each rule, at accepting each rule's relative importance (some rules are more important than others), and at knowing the tolerated ways to change the rules. The acceptable way to review those rules and rewrite them is called renegotiating. It is built on the premise that change is a normal part of the growth pattern and it happens easiest through discussion and with intentionality.

Effective parents start using and teaching about negotiating and renegotiating early in life. They make, and then consciously change, the rules about when children can go outside, whose house they can visit, and when they must be home. Transitional rules like those will change a dozen times during the growing years. Our skill at renegotiation determines how peaceful those changes (and those years) will be.

My husband and I attended a parenting class in the hope of gaining insight into raising our daughters. They were presenting challenges to us. At the end of the class I had at least gone from the valley (or the pits) to the plain, learning that other parents had the same problems and that there were no pat answers.

She's right. There are no pat answers. But there are skills for developing useful answers for the moment. In one sense every chapter in this book relates to how effective parents negotiate and renegotiate. You might even say that the heart of parental effectiveness is not rigidity and firmness but how—and how well—change is handled.

That leads to another question: "What's subject to change?" Will rules change? Will parents change? Will children change? Will choices change? Yes, yes, yes, and yes—all of the above. No one and nothing is exempt from change in an effective family. The same thing goes for the ineffective family—only it denies the changing.

Effective parents underline that point.

From Michigan: *We feel strongly that you cannot treat each child the same. They are so different and they have such different needs at different times in their lives.*

An Iowa dad offers a glimpse of jetlike change in his child: *We sent Joanie to dance class. After a while she decided she didn't care for it too much. We didn't force her to go anymore.*

And here's a picture of life in Arizona and how the extended family was included at change moments by this effective mom: *Our son was confirmed this year. We celebrated the event with a buffet supper. Tom's mother came from Des Moines and old friends joined us from Houston. The couple who stood at the baptismal font with him drove over from the other side of town to see him reaffirm his faith. The rites of passage are important. We share them joyfully with people we love. It is an important part of our family and something that is worth the effort to make these occasions of change special.*

Effective parents can make daring approaches to inevitable change with surprising side benefits:

I believe that our interest in our two older ones during high school shaped our younger children. With much prayer, little sense, less money, and the Holy Spirit's leading, my wife and I, with another couple, led a weekly youth group in our home. The younger kids usually participated or were at least "there." We all grew closer in our relationship with Jesus and with the 10 or 15 other young people who became an important part of our extended family. The younger ones may have been in the way but were accepted by the other youth and were particularly included by their older brothers.

Anyone with kids knows how much change has to happen for an older brother to include little ones in the kind of association this letter outlined. The report features super kids, super parents—and supersonic change!

One important caution from a Kansas dad:

It is important for us to not give up the values we believe are important. More than that we need to hold onto them in difficult times. But when the old systems are replaced with the newer and better values, we have to be able to let the old ones go.

Right! Effective parents do not change the life-building basics. But woe to the parent who cannot discriminate between what is essential to life and what is a stubborn dad's slanted opinion.

An effective Missouri father helps with that. He has a good approach to the change he has experienced in the family—and even on some that is to come:

*I do not have all the neat sayings, quotes, and words of wisdom of a Father-Knows-Best person. But I know my kids. And I know what they are doing. I want to be part of their growing. For me the best years of my children's lives will be from birth through high school. For **me!** I want those years. The best years for them are after high school, when they leave to build their own futures. I won't mind waving goodbye. After all, my wife and I got married because of each other, not them. As we raise these kids and send them off, we will still have one another **and** will have had the best years of our kids' lives. It's exciting and fulfilling to be a parent. And fun. But you need to work at it.*

There was also a letter from a father as great as that Missouri one. This second letter differs only in perspective. At the far edge of nuclear-family life, looking back and around, he reflects as the kids are about to leave. We heard a sentence or so from him before. Here's some more, appropriate to this chapter:

We are going through a tough period now. I was laid off from a good job 18 months ago and haven't had a regular paycheck for a long time. I'm enrolled in a good school and I hope to start a new career next fall. But we are essentially living on our good credit history, trying to race the clock against bankruptcy. Cutting back and cutting out has put a lot of pressure on our family— wondering what will happen. But we've developed a strong faith and God has surely sustained us. During the last two years we have learned to pray aloud together. It has helped the whole family open up and trust in God's guidance for our lives. We've dropped out of a very secure middle-class life-style and stepped into a far more secure Christian faith.

That family not only talks about change. They live it!

In later chapters we will deal with some of the apprehensions you may be feeling now. Where does spirituality fit into this discussion? How do we make sure we aren't just falling for what is the latest? How do we develop—or improve—our renegotiation skills?

For the moment don't worry about those questions. For the moment focus on the message of this chapter. Change is here. It is here to stay. Don't be afraid of it. Make decisions. But be an effective parent. Be ready to change those decisions. In the process keep the whole family involved. Especially do that in the areas where absolute decisions are hard to come by—like in the subject of the next chapter. It's a toughie.

Stay-at-Home Mom: Yes? No?

◆

I continued to teach until our oldest started kindergarten. Up to that time the boys went to the baby-sitter during the day. When I quit teaching, it was a big adjustment. I still miss it.

—An Ohio Mother

I have been a stay-at-home mom since our daughter was born. This has been a financial challenge to us. But we wanted our children home with their mother while they were young.

—An Illinois Mother

I drop my child at the baby-sitter and go to work. I'm picky about where she stays. It's tough being single.

—An Indiana Mother

One area of enormous change over the past 30 years is the world of stay-at-home moms. This is especially true in the world of our youngest mothers. As late as the 1960s, almost any church women's group could meet in the morning or the afternoon, as long as the meeting adjourned before school was out. Not many women's groups met in the evenings. Moms stayed at home. People then, men and women alike, would likely have added, " ... where they belong." That's the way it was. Was.

Now, according to a survey by the National Association for the Education of Young Children, not only do most moms work at jobs outside the home, 28% of them send their preschoolers to child-care centers, a percentage up from 13% in 1977. Big jump. An additional 19% use their relatives to care for their children during the day. Add the percentages and you find a near majority of America's families—47%—place their preschool children in the care of someone else while mom heads off to the workplace. The number grows year by year. Will it ever stop? Should it?

Those dramatic figures still don't give the complete picture. There are camouflaged variations that make it seem like the 1950 pattern of family is still in operation. But it isn't. Here's one deceptive anecdote:

> *We had our first child in 1982. Myra worked the third shift while I tended Marie during those evening hours. It was difficult and my patience wore thin, but we survived.*

I think you should add their story to the 47% of homes in which relatives or day-care centers are prime attendants of children. If you did, then what's the percentage?

And how would you classify homes where Mom is always present (sound good?) because that's where she does demanding work like running a business from the dining room table or making a saleable product in the basement. In which world does she belong?

If I were to guess the real number of 1990 mothers who are just like their 1950 predecessors, I doubt if they would constitute 25% of the whole. Shifting the focus to the city, especially the inner city, those numbers would move up into the 90th percentile. High-blown rhetoric to the contrary, there aren't many stay-at-home moms in the United States today. Even those who look like stay-at-homes do not pass under examination. The last few sentences are not opinion. They are fact.

Do effective parents have feelings on this subject? Oh, yes. But there are major differences among them. Concerning stay-at-home moms (their term, by the way, not mine), they are split.

The majority of the effective parents, about 60%, have made an intentional decision that mother should stay at home. That makes them different from the others in our society. They know that. But they still think moms belong at home as the children grow.

My wife is a wonderful mother. We both know that the most important place for her

*at this time is at home. She has been there
since we began the family. We feel the home
is where the Lord wants her.*

Others agree with their conclusion, but few
feel that a stay-at-home mom is the will of God.
They explain it differently. One mother puts is this
way:

*The bottom line is that we are a normal fam-
ily. I am here for my children. I have chosen not to work outside of my home because
I want to be here. I sit at the kitchen table
with cookies and milk waiting for their bus
or their car. If they want to talk, we do. If
they don't, we don't. I love them dearly and
know God does too.*

Lots of important "I-messages" (we'll explain
that term later) in her views. She accepts responsibility for their decisions. There's power in that
paragraph.

Another agrees with her:

*Even before we married, we set up many of
the goals and rules by which we live now.
We decided early that the only way to have
children is to raise them ourselves. We took
this one step further—we decided to home
school our children. Obviously, we don't
have a lot of luxuries, extravagant recre-
ational things, or vacations. And we spend
extra time with our family. Having less
money makes it easy to say no to such things*

*as cable TV and Nintendo, both of which
pull families away from interacting.*

There's that word "decide" again. Actually it
is at the heart of this chapter. Decide comes from a
Latin root that means "to cut." Couples who live
out the excerpts have made some powerful "cuts."
And they claim them! This mom does too:

*We feel that being a stay-at-home mom is
the most important thing that I can do. I like
being here when they come home, finding
out about their day. No one can take my
place. The longer you are with your kids, the
more you instill **your** values and **your**
beliefs.*

And one more: *Although Dan's mother
worked part time, she was there for her family. Our family goals are similar except I
believe I should be available to my children
all the time—something that is not really
popular. I have never worked outside the
home.*

The last five excerpts represent one of the two
clearest (there are some vague ones) positions on
the question of whether moms should stay at
home. Though few state that staying home is what
God would want, I get the feeling most think He
smiles approvingly.

The opposite position is just as clearly stated
by effective parents. It is maintained with no
apparent twinge of conscience and was apparently

reached without undue struggle. Their reasons for going along with the national norm are one or more of three: (1) The mothers feel they are gifted in a career direction. (2) They feel their children are better cared for with the supporting assistance of a third party—whom they have carefully selected. Or, (3) Their salary is important to their family.

Elements of all three can be sensed in this note from a medical doctor, the mother of three, who says: *I chose my medical specialty because of regular hours and the few late-night emergencies. Although I have a fairly high commitment to my work, my family is always my first priority. At times I've considered the possibility of being a full-time mom, but I lose patience with kids and become frustrated. I really believe that it is better for me to work because work is a good outlet and an area of relative predictability compared to the demands of children.*

Her clearly stated view is held by a large number of women/wives/mothers who have adopted career goals during their mothering moment. I'm guessing (but with lots of supporting evidence) that as more women become lawyers, engineers, doctors, managers, pilots, bankers, and other specialists, this style of mothering will increase as well.

In my later interviews and through the questionnaires, I pressed all the working moms (single, married, those who want to work, those who must) for more comment. They gave it. Much surfaced. I sensed it would be wrong to say they have a less caring attitude toward their children or that work was a thoughtless choice. Whether you agree or disagree with what they do, the choice was made by parenting teams (singles too) who are recognized as effective.

But let's go on to a not-so-clear aspect of this picture. While it's true that mothers stay at home among the majority of effective parents, even that majority is not as unified as it appears. There are variations within the classification of stay-at-homes that make you wonder whether the term is accurate.

One variation of the majority position says you can be a stay-at-home mom and continue working full time. Sometimes this means changing work hours, or working only until the baby is a little older, or working until a second child is born.

We had our first child in 1982. Jane worked the third shift and I tended the baby during the evening hours. Jane stopped working when we had a second child in 1984. She stayed home to be a full-time mother. This was a mutual decision.

Maybe Jane should be called a stay-at-home-later mom?

A variation of this approach features the same decision, but it kicks in later in the family's life:

The big change in our family came in 1989. After more than 24 years of being a two-career family, Bill and I decided I would quit my job and devote full time to home-making and parenting. We had four children and there seemed to be some disequi-librium in the ranks. The pull to be home with the children and devote a more focused effort on their growth and well-being became impossible to ignore.

Where might she fit in the stay-at-home ver-sus the work-outside sweepstakes? Pro? Con?

A third variation is the same as the second, only the decision is not to quit and come home when the children are somewhat grown but to go full time at that stage:

Financially we decided to do without some things to allow Louanne to be a full-time mother when the children were small. It's only been the last couple years when she has worked full time. Even so, she still takes our daughter to school.

That last sentence apparently makes a differ-ence to the dad who wrote the report.

Don't think I've spun off all the variations of stay-at-home moms. There's still the largest vari-ety to come. I don't know whether to call this vari-ation a part-time-full-time-working mother or a part-time-full-time-stay-at-home mom. Here are three illustrations of what I found:

> *As soon as our daughter was born, I became a full-time mother/wife/homemaker. When she was 18 months old, I returned to work but only for one day a week as an RN.*

> Or, from a dad, the report that *I worked the day shift and my wife worked afternoons and evenings. We felt it important to have either a dad or mom home with the kids. It wasn't too hard on me. I learned to cook suppers and clean up afterwards. The kids were young and had early bedtimes. So by 8 p.m. my day was done and I still had some time for myself.*

> Or, *Lynn is a domestic engineer and a very busy person. She does child care for five children ages eight months to two years in our home and also mothers our four children ages five to 11 years. This helps supplement our family income.*

See how it works? These mothers offer the appearance of being stay-at-home moms, but they keep their hand in work in a lot of ways. Some do so discreetly, and part time, with a reason. Others flip-flop child care with the father, making sure there's always one parent guarding the nest. Still others bring a full-time job into the home, doing the work there, in addition to another full-time commitment. Stay-at-home mom? She is probably a very tired stay-at-home mom.

Not all varieties are as transparent as those cited. Money-making side vocations in crafts, sewing, bookkeeping, baking, tutoring, music, and dance lessons can blend into the woodwork of life without being seen for what they are. Sometimes the children even pitch in to help these go-to-work-at-home moms. It's hard to call these examples of stay-at-home moms.

In presenting this data I am offering no personal judgement. These pages are prepared for and by effective parents as they come at the issue of whether mothers ought to stay at home. Remember, again, that the excerpts are not from randomly selected homes. They are comments, observations, and insights from those nominated as effective parents. And they have more variations to share.

Ever heard of a no-I-don't-have-an-outside-or-inside-job-stay-at-home mom, who looks like one, but isn't? She certainly generates no additional income through her activity. You decide whether she fits in the stay-at-home category:

I am fortunate to be a stay-at-home mom. As such I work in the school cafeteria and help out when needed. I serve on committees, the PTL board, a church guild, and chauffeur everyone to their various activities. Someday soon I will need to get back to work part time, but I'm glad I've been home these past 12 years.

That stay-at-home mom doesn't seem to stay at home very much. She renders all kinds of useful service to her family and community in areas far beyond what anyone would call parenting. As a pastor, I daily depend upon support from this kind of dynamic mother. Without her, much good would not happen. Schools and volunteer organizations would be devastated without this kind of mom. When she finally goes back into the marketplace to work, it will probably seem tame as her life eases into the slower lanes of full-time work. Right now she is a high-speed, stay-at-home look-alike! But is she a stay-at-home mom? What do you think?

So, what should **you** do? Work for hire? Stay at home?

I think the "authorities" I am presenting—all recognized, effective Christians—would urge you to make your own decision. "Pray," they would say. "And think." Both. Do both constantly. Over and over. Alternately. Simultaneously, if you can. Think and pray. Pray and think.

We'll discuss the place of prayer in the lives of effective parents in another chapter. It's an important aspect—and more—of effective parenting. For now, note that effective parents place prayer at the point of first impulse when an issue is important. They really believe that James 5:16 passage that prayer " ... is powerful and effective."

They follow Luther's advice to pray like everything depends on God and then work like everything depends on us. That's one thing they say. The other is, "Use your head; think."

Effective parents did not become effective by being impulsive or by giving in to knee-jerk reactions. Their approach to problems is much more calculated. When a decision moment comes, they pray first. But then they reflectively analyze their situation, taking as much time as is needed—like Nehemiah did. In the interim they develop a plan—like Nehemiah did. An effective parent plan—maybe that's one reason they are effective.

From Arkansas comes an insight into how a family made sure mom would not need to work for financial reasons. This father writes:

> *Families need to be organized and concerned about stewardship. Parents have the responsibility of managing time and money to the glory of God and the blessing of family members. In our family we attempt to limit diversion in our professional, personal, and church lives. This means avoiding working too hard, getting overcommitted to recreational activities (parent and child alike), and saying no sometimes to church-related things. We also keep track of where our money goes. Nothing throws a wrench into a healthy family quicker than financial stress. This doesn't mean we are slaves to our budget. It means we strive to help our-*

selves make decisions with as much infor-mation as possible.

That family decided (there's that word, again) the mother would not work. In making their decision they reviewed and revised their lifestyle so she would not have to work. Sound financial planning was a key element in their thoughtful approach to whether their mom would have to work outside the home for income purposes.

Another from Michigan: *I was fortunate enough to stay at home and be a full-time mother. Had I been working, I don't think I would have had the patience to deal with our children. A child's values are shaped in the first few years, and I sure feel better knowing my children were shaped by me and not the values of another. It means some sacrifice in material things and putting my career on hold, but I wouldn't change those years at home with my children for any-thing.*

Count the first person singular pronouns in the preceding paragraph. That mother, (1) evalu-ated herself, (2) took responsibility for her situation, (3) reached a conclusion, and (4) acted on it. Effective parents don't spend time taking potshots at others, or offering sweeping generalized solutions, or stampeding in directions others determine. They make the case for what they are doing, give the reasons, and act.

One last letter, from Minnesota, of how a couple made their decision about the stay-at-home question long before their baby's birth. They illustrate the pattern of prayerful thoughtfulness many—(most?)—effective parents follow.

When we married after dating for about two years, we agreed we were one. That included our finances and careers. We do not have "mine" and "yours." We are both pharmacists and have worked for four years. We agreed that when we had children, I would quit and be a full-time mom. For that reason, even when I was working full time, we lived off of one paycheck. The other went into savings and was used for special things such as vacations. We felt fortunate to have those four years to get to know each other, to travel, and to save money before we had our first child. Then our lives changed dramatically. Our children became our priority.

Plan for the future and work your plan. Effective parents are at their best doing that.

Want to try an effective parent approach to this question for your life? You can. Prayerfully search God's Word. Evaluate your present life situation. Do you have choices? (Careful now!) Is it possible to expand those choices? How long, and at what cost, might that be done? Can you discuss your views on this subject with your partner? Are you ready to do that? Begin with those questions and then press on.

Is there a child in the picture already? More than one? Do they have special needs? What kind of support can you expect from your extended family and from any larger community to which you are attached? Are there choices in those environments?

The questions in the last few paragraphs are basic to whether your life situation is better blessed by being a working mother or a stay-at-home mom. Answering them will help you make good and useful decisions. Go at them thoughtfully, depending on the Holy Spirit's guidance. Don't forget prayer.

I have one more thing to share. It is so rich in understanding, and honest in expression, that it must be included. There's no point in citing the state from which the author writes, for in one form or another her thoughts are nationwide. She became a stay-at-home mom after a long period of professional service outside the home. Now she reports:

The first year of my "big change" was a struggle for me. I missed work and the professional affiliations that went with it. But I discovered I could continue to work in a peripheral way at home and began doing some professional writing. This, along with an occasional day of clinical nursing, kept me from feeling like I wasn't falling too far behind in my professional pursuits. I can always catch up when the children are a little older. But the real growth and source of pride and accomplishment has come from watching our children flourish under my new direction. Since I am no longer assigning the majority of my parenting work to other people, I am taking credit for the rewards and successes of our children's accomplishments. The credit really belongs to them, but I can be there and witness their success (and failures) first hand and offer congratulations (or condolences) in a timely fashion and also supply the hugs and kisses for well-deserved accomplishments.

As you read the other chapters of this book, flip back to this letter and see how many of the elements of effective parenting she dropped into that one paragraph. It's awesome.

So where are we? Here: Effective parents as a group offer no pat answers to questions of stay at home or work outside. Different effective parents do different things for different reasons at different times. There is no common action pattern. But there is a common heart. It thumps out love in every beat. And there is a soul, too, as the next chapter will show.

In God They Trust

Every year His parents went to Jerusalem for the Feast of the Passover. When He was twelve years old, they went up to the Feast, according to their custom (Luke 2:41–42).
—A Report of an Effective Family, cir. 12 A.D.

Don't hide your faith. Let your children know you have a strong faith and practice it. Go to church and Sunday school with your kids. Don't just drop them off.
—A Missouri Mother

I find it hard to imagine what it would be like to raise our children without the knowledge and understanding of God's wonderful plan for our lives.
—A Delaware Father

I would expect a chapter on spirituality in a book about effective Christian parents. You too? Don't worry. There is, but not because I decided there would be. As with all the other subjects this book discusses, spirituality is included because effective parents willed it so.

Spirituality is a significant subject for effective parents. It is integral to their lives. I'll get out of the way and let them develop the subject as they want, even if they seem to ignore things I believe are very important.

Let's start with this: Among effective parents, spirituality is not a wishy-washy commitment to a vague and ill-defined set of religious beliefs. Their spirituality has content. Bone and muscle. There's nothing vague or remote about their faith. Who says? These four and more.

- *Two people under Christ make this family work. It only takes one saboteur to wreck things. Oh, the mistakes! Those I see with hindsight—and I'm aware of so many that are not yet revealed. I cannot comprehend how those without Christ continue.*

- *From the time Steve and I had our first date until we married, it was just short of 10 years. Our relationship was off and on over those years. But I always knew he was the man I wanted to marry. God had work to do in each of our lives before we were ready for each other. It was definitely worth waiting for the right man at the right time. I think the foundation for an effective parental team is marrying a person who is a growing and committed Christian.*

- *Our belief in God and the importance of developing a personal relationship with Jesus Christ is a binding factor that supports our family. Our faith and our church are focal points to rally around.*

- *We believe that to have a strong family you must have a good foundation. The obvious foundation is Christ. He is at the center. Another element of the foundation is the relationship between man and wife—Christianity practiced. We are fortunate that with every passing day our relationship gets stronger. This does not just happen.*

Are they Christian? No doubt! Do they practice their faith? Yes! Of special note is that they practice their faith in three distinct areas of applied spirituality, two of them included in this note from an Indiana husband:

Christ is the center of our lives. We pray together. We study God's Word together. We feel totally comfortable talking about who God is and what He has done for us.

The two? Bible study and prayer. The third, not included as such in this letter, is family devotions. But it shows up so often elsewhere that there's no question that these are the Big Three in the effective family's application of Christian beliefs.

That first one, Bible study, could have been missed. It was seldom specific. Here and there it was alluded to, as this Oregon mom says:

I never read how-to books or belonged to a discussion group for young moms. I have always relied on God, and past experiences, for guidance. I still do today—although I read the Bible and other Christian material and go to hear Christian speakers. I believe we need to know Christ personally and seek His will in all areas of our lives.

Did you note how the subject of Bible study showed up? It just slid into the sentence. Without forcing others to conform to their practices, effective parents state what they do and then leave it up to you. There is, of course, within their correspondence and conversation, a lot of encouragement toward Sunday school, Bible classes, and all forms of Christian education, none of which can be done without Bible study. But exuberant, specific demand for Bible reading? It's not there. It is assumed.

I'll bypass prayer for the moment to mention the third expression of spirituality among effective parents: the devotional life. A Wisconsin father states:

What's the secret of our home and marriage? The answer is God. Marie and I both learned from our parents that God must come first in our life. In our home we don't

*eat until we talk to God, and we don't leave
the table without family devotions. Our personal motto is, "Give God the first hour of
every day, the first day of every week, and
the first dime of every dollar." That has kept
us all together and out of serious trouble. It
has enabled all our children to be dedicated
workers, college graduates, faithful church
members, and responsible adults.*

From Ohio comes a similar report of commitment to family devotions:

*We have family devotions after supper. After
devotions, and before we give thanks, each
of us shares a blessing we received from God
that day. We try to be Christian by example.
We can preach as we want, but if our hearts
and lives don't reflect what we say, we
receive no respect as parents.*

Some older national studies report that only
about 5% of Christian families have family devotions. That's not true among effective families. It
appears to me that 80% have some kind of regular
family devotions. They do their devoting with
intentionality and with an awareness of other
things that contribute to a devotional life in the
family. So that family devotions can happen, effective parents make sure their families are together,
in one place, regularly. Then, while gathered
together, effective parents insist that conversation,
involving everyone, happens! (The need for those
two basics is maintained with such vigor by effec-

tive parents that later chapters in this book largely focus on each of them.) The fact that they are gathered and are talking sets the stage for a devotional time together. It's as simple as that.

Young families need to make an early decision on the question of family devotions. Don't make the moment too ponderous. Maybe sing a song or tell a story or read a bit of good material. Then give everyone a chance to comment, observe, or respond. Not long. But involving. And what will happen? In time the devotional moment will become natural and the involvement will expand. But first, parents must make a decision.

Now—another of an effective parent's spiritual decisions—prayer.

Prayer often showed up early in the relations of effective parents. Looking back, one mother wrote about her courting days:

We spent a great deal of time in prayer about our upcoming marriage. We knew it would be difficult at best to bring our two families together into one family unit. But we also knew that if we truly sought God's will for us and our children—and we were committed to doing things His way—He would honor our desire and steadfastness and enable us to be successful in building the family we visualized and He wanted for us. So we prayed.

A west-coast father adds his experience: *Since my teenage years, I knew I wanted to get married and have a family. I didn't realize it would take so long. At the age of 29 I was still single. It's tough for a shy guy to meet people. But I had learned about praying from my dad and had practiced it in Vietnam. So, back home, I prayed for a spouse. Not only did I meet her but we were married within a year. We have since been blessed with four daughters. It's been a busy home.*

Three more effective parents add their insight on the subject of prayer.

One of the most important things about parenting is your relationship with God. If you don't spend enough time with Him in prayer, you can't know what He expects of you as a parent. Pray for your children at least once a day. And don't forget the mate God has chosen for you.

An effective family strives to make Christ the center. It is a daily walk—fresh every day—requiring thought and planning. Above all, it requires prayer. Our heavenly Father promises to listen.

I pray. I prayed at night for God to protect my children at school. I prayed that God would protect them from themselves and help them make good grades and learn.

After high school I prayed that God would help them stand up to the adversities of college. After college I prayed that God would help them find good jobs, faithful partners, and that God would teach them to be good partners. In the morning as I go to work at 6:25 a.m., I pray that God will protect my children all day.

I felt from the first that effective parents would probably say something about prayer, but I was not prepared for the intensity of their interest or the volume of their comments. Both are there. From coast to coast effective couples believe in prayer and its power—and practice what they believe.

Effective parents believe in going to church too.

We go to church every Sunday. I get up early and prepare a nice breakfast. The girls always wear dresses. We feel they can wear a dress for a few hours on Sunday. They have the rest of the week to wear pants.

Another, just as direct: *We worship in church and attend Sunday school regularly.*

Do the kids share their parents' enthusiasm for worship? What do you think? One dad reports:

During our children's growing years they complained about attending church. We explained that was the way it was. When they got to elementary school, I said that if they didn't want to go, we, instead, would dress in our Sunday best and sit in the living room on chairs during the Sunday school and church hours because that was the Lord's time. I never had any takers. Most children sit engrossed before a TV set or movie for hours, so why not attend church? I think it might be a convenient excuse for parents.

No comment from me.

Just to give the complete picture, one effective twosome, with a newer commitment to the church, is just now picking up on worship. They don't beat around the bush.

We are still learning the importance of having a church family and of Christian fellowship. Neither one of us had a particularly strong Christian background.

But they are learning. And guess what? While the mom and dad are learning, so are the kids.

As spiritual as effective parents may be, they still live in a real world. Two mothers share lovely pictures of how life at its worst intersects with spirituality at its best:

From Wisconsin the words of a mom standing in both worlds who says, *Several weeks ago I had a spiritual experience involving my son. He was injured at baseball practice and I took him to the emergency room where we learned that his spleen had rup-*

tured. That same night he had surgery and required three pints of blood. During the surgery I realized I would gladly have taken his place if that were possible. While I was sharing the feeling with him the day after the surgery, I not only realized how much I loved him, but—probably for the first time in my life—I truly realized just how much Christ loved us when He willingly died for us. When I told my son, he gave me a hug. I think that's the closest we've ever felt toward each other.

A mother from Indiana adds her real/spiritual report: *Having one baby was fun, like playing house. Two were more difficult. We had been through all this before and a feeling of drudgery set in. I found I was always tired, impatient, unable to control myself, let alone our children and their emerging personalities. The awareness of my inability to be the kind of relaxed, nurturing parent I wanted to be often caused me to go to bed weeping in frustration and guilt. I remember my husband assuring me that God forgave my sins of impatience and harshness in dealing with two small boys. Later, when more children arrived, I realized that I was trying to be god over them, controlling their lives, and experiencing the inability of the task. I prayed to experience the healing power of the Gospel in our family. The Lord heard and began to answer my prayer. I had been content to know Jesus as Savior. I began to trust Him as Lord and lead my children to know Him. The emphasis changed from "doing a job for Him" to "letting Him do His work in me."*

Variations of her pilgrimlike progress—but only variations—were offered again and again.

So, then, what's the point to this chapter? Just what the title states. Effective parents face the real world trusting in God—trusting in the God who established families and sacrificed His own Son out of love for them, to guide them through every challenge. They show their trust through Bible study, family devotions, and prayer, even as they nurture their trust in the promises God gives them in His Word and the forgiveness He showers upon them in His Sacrament. That's not a very complicated way to go at faith. But it sure works. Trusting in what God has done for them in Christ, they seem to keep their spirituality simple—and at the center. There's not much more to report. Nor need there be.

I tested the written convictions of my effective parents on a panel of preschool parents, all striving to become effective parents in their own right. Their reaction? Agreement. Large-scale agreement.

Spirituality in our home is at the center. Children model their behavior on ours from the start. That's why our 18-month- and

*three-year-old are really into forgiveness.
We have a song we sing every time we say
we're sorry or want to forgive someone. We
can do this only because we know Jesus forgives us constantly. And prayer? I pray
every day. I'm sure that's the only way to
survive. We try hard to deal with morality,
kindness, and understanding to others. It's
the parents' job. We are to teach our children about God, raise them in a Christian
home, and set an example of Christian
behavior. Christian parenting is based on
Christ, our driving force.*

Take the time to dig around in that collage of
comments for practical suggestions about developing and applying spiritual values in a home with
tiny tots.

Betty, the mother of a young child, adds her
own bright spirituality—and an understanding of
how spirituality works—saying:

*Andy and I took the class "Right from the
Start" at church. We learned that the parent is the child's first model of what a loving,
giving, forgiving God is like. In developing
the child's concept of unconditional love,
and the child's ability to trust that love, parents set down a strong foundation for later
spiritual growth. Just as with the parents'
love, the parents' spirituality will be infectious.*

One response to Betty's last sentence might be, "That remains to be seen." And it will be if teaching can bring it to the fore.

Teaching—our next subject.

Teaching, Discipline, and the School-in-Our-Home

We always had guidelines. They knew what was expected of them and how far they could go. It is important that kids know what is expected of them and that you love them no matter what.

—A Nebraska Dad

Discipline was something big in my life. It is now big in my children's lives. They have rules to live by.

—An Ohio Dad

The home is any child's first school. By extension, trained and certified or not, Mom and Dad are everyone's first teachers. In the effective home (and in every home that wants to be) they teach the fundamentals of life. The learning happens easiest and best when the teachers intentionally teach—and the students are ready, willing, and eager to learn. Even when moms and dads deny the educational opportunity of the home and are indiffer-

93

ent to their role, they still are teaching. It's just that they are teaching the wrong stuff!

In my research, all newer parents clearly recognized that the home is a place of learning and they are the teachers. The most recurring words, sprinkled throughout their comments, were teach, learn, guide, lead, instruct—all words educators use. No matter the subject, one or more of those verbs found their way into most sentences. I do not know what level of awareness lay behind their use. Whatever, I'm sure this chapter will increase it.

Do their seniors, the proven effective parents, agree that the home is a school and that parents are the teachers? You bet they do! They do with one important addition: Proven effective parents accent that home teaching, at its best, is team teaching. Team. Usually—but not always—that team is a husband and wife. Usually. But not always.

I first noticed the accent on team teaching in older parents' comments about how kids intentionally try to drive wedges between parental partners. The parents saw through that ploy because it was nothing new to them. They had tried the same thing themselves. One remembered:

I had no doubt whose side Mom or Dad would be on in any argument I might have with the other. They presented a united front, and woe betide the child that tried to play one against the other!

A modern parent shows how little things have changed when she writes:

The children know and accept the fact that their father and I discuss everything and that we make decisions together. It's important the children know they cannot play one parent against the other. All children will try this, but in our situation this would be very bad. The children of one parent could easily play that parent against the stepparent.

Just in case the last paragraph is not specific enough, try this one:

Kids need to know that Mom and Dad are united. There's to be no sneaking behind Dad's back to get something from Mom or vice-versa. Occasionally they slip one by us, but we usually find out and confront them.

Reread that last sentence and focus on the final three words. They may sound harsh, but the truth is that intentional and studied confrontation is teaching at its best. At its best, confrontation is a great entry point to renegotiation and forgiveness. Healing words.

Effective parents are determined to not only maintain a unified front but are determined to actually be unified. A commitment to be the team they agreed to be on their wedding day is a hidden strength of parental effectiveness. A Kansas team member lays it out saying:

Millie and I present a united front before the children. When, in fact, we disagree, we discuss the matter privately.

Ditto from Ohio, Michigan, and Colorado:

- *I believe the most important part of the family puzzle is cooperation, especially on the part of my wife and me.*

- *Rena and I actually agree on most everything. We say the same things at the same time, which is scary. We think alike. We love each other and convey this to the children.*

- *When necessary my husband and I discuss what we both think about a matter and then come to an agreeable decision. It has not been our practice to pray aloud about these matters. I regret this.*

Those sentences prove again that effective family issues connect and mix. The concerns of the last two chapters permeate this one, especially the last three statements. The concerns are clearest in the last two sentences of the third. Pause for a moment and test that out. In so doing you will reinforce the key understanding of the connection between all the subjects in this book.

At first, acting as a team may not seem important to younger parents. But it is. A common view of child-rearing and establishing common goals in training are crucial. Young parents soon find out that even the littlest ones become skilled at playing one parent against the other—if they are allowed to do so. Right? After a correction by one parent, the little sweetheart will tearfully head for the other parent, climb into his or her arms and plead innocence. Now what does Parent 2 do? That tear-stained moment is filled with educational possibilities—and pregnant with danger for the team.

The best handling of that predicament is not developed in that moment. The best handling happens weeks, even months, before.

Dan and I agreed that we would not let the children make one of us laugh in a situation that the other is taking seriously. We would not undercut each other, even if we felt our partner was off base.

Those are wise words from a young mother. If the parents have discussed the standards and have decided to back each other in moments like that, everyone in the family ends up being blessed. If they have further agreed that they will take final action only after consulting together when new situations surface, the children will quickly learn that they must always deal with both parents.

So, make these three decisions:

- *We will agree on standards.*

- *We will consistently support each other on what we have set until a change has been negotiated.*

97

- *We will normally take no final actions without consultation.*

That's team teaching—the kind that makes teaching a lot easier.

And what happens when effective parents don't or can't agree. Maybe even disagree? Those questions shift the focus from decision content to partnership style. This Missouri mother speaks for dozens:

> *As husband and wife we do not always agree. However, it is important how we "disagree" in front of the children. Children learn by seeing their parents interact with one another and with others. We strive to teach our children by our actions that they should treat one another as they want to be treated.*

That's another of those interconnecting observations, going back to the chapter on love. Love of others builds from self-love. Proper self-love, in turn, grows out of Christ's love for us.

Adding it all up, effective parents are team teachers. They protect and defend their team's integrity by standing up for each other. Because they do not always agree, they develop a means for disagreeing with each other. They do not inhibit the educational process in the home. Organizing their teaching team is the first step that effective parents take in developing a good school-in-our-home.

Another thing effective parents tell us about the school-in-our-home is that they have schedules and a curriculum. In many ways these two are the same thing.

The word *curriculum* comes from the Latin word (*curricula*) for a race track—an oval with a beginning and an end—around which horses raced. The *curricula* controlled the thundering, hurly-burly of horses in high speed by keeping them on a predetermined, controlled path. The school-in-our-home curriculum is similar. It establishes a track to follow and sets a schedule for doing so.

> *From the time the children were little, we have kept them on a schedule. The schedule changes as they get older, but we believe in structure and consistency.*

In those words a midwestern mother tells us of their home's educational scheduling. It begins with feeding and naps and goes from there. An Oregon dad further explains the interconnection of schedule and curriculum saying:

> *Lynn keeps the children in routines and on schedule when it comes to meals, naps, and bedtime. Children need regularity in their lives—something they can depend on day to day. They know what to expect. There is little room to negotiate at those times. This*

eliminates arguments, which—in turn—reduces the number of "headaches" for parents.

When parents have a schedule for the life events of little children, they ought to have an idea of what they want to teach via that schedule. High on the list must be teaching self-control and social skills. What kind of self-control and which social skills? How about self-control in the area of a social skill such as politeness? A Missouri father-teacher shows us how:

Friends always remark how polite our children are. There's no trick to that. That's how we are, all day, every day, at our house. When neighborhood kids are over and demand, "Push me in the swing" or "I want a drink," we ask them to include a "please" in their request. They may have to force themselves to say it, but they know that Donna and I won't assist them any other way. Parents set the example by having a standard and maintaining it day in and day out.

Sounds simple the way he explains it. Home-schools teach about relationships and social skills best when the subject standards are clearly stated and consistently maintained. That's another way of saying that in the best school-in-our-home there are rules.

Having and using rules may sound negative to some but not to effective parents. Not even to their younger pioneers. Good rules have a positive.

We have rules. We make sure they are good rules. We follow them.

So writes a mother of a child not yet a year old. Do effective parents, younger or older, agree on the importance of rules? Yes. Yes, indeed. From Ohio comes a story of how clearly stated—and firmly maintained—home-school rules set the stage for teaching a life value:

We faced the struggle of church and Sunday school attendance. It certainly would have been easier not to go, especially when some of the five children were always complaining they didn't want to go. For a while I dreaded Sunday morning upheavals and arguments. But those died down and disappeared when the announcement was made—and meant— that our family worshiped together in church every Sunday and that the decision was not debatable.

The "teachers" tied a rule to one of their school-in-our-home teaching objectives: Families worship each week. Together. Im-plicit is the hope that their children would take this family decision out into life, making "the family rule" a personal value.

Many younger parents come at the question of weekly worship early on—before it is a problem.

They take the children with them to church from the first.

We sit in the front row. There's less distraction and more action, one father wrote.

It doesn't take many Sundays of gentle guidance to help even the smallest child learn how to act in church. But, by the same token, children will act no different in church than they do elsewhere.

Don't expect a child to sit still in worship when they are allowed to run wild in every other situation, writes a great young teaching mother. She adds: *We teach our children how to act in church by how we let them act in a store or in their grandparent's home.*

The great teacher makes the point that the real educational concern is not, "How do we teach our children to act properly in church?" but "How are our children to act anywhere?"

Support for that comes from an Illinois mother:

I feel great pride that God has given me a wonderful husband and three beautiful and healthy children. My responsibility, together with my husband, is to raise them the best way we can. We must not only love and respect them, but nurture them in a Christian moral lifestyle that has so much gone by the wayside.

The word nurture jumped out at me from that comment. You too? Nurture is an educator's word. It's a word-picture featuring a gardener who weeds around a plant and works plant food into the soil—and then the plant does the growing. Two actions: Gardeners nurture; plants grow. That's how education happens in the school-in-our-home as well.

What if "the plant" is difficult or won't cooperate? Go back a few paragraphs. In cases like that, *set rules appropriate to the age of your children and stick to them,* say our effective parents. Is that the same as discipline? I think so.

Discipline is different from punishment. I don't believe in punishing children. Nor do our effective parents. They feel raw punishment is pointless. It responds to some base need within a parent and makes education more difficult. It has no point. Discipline (which means "to make a disciple—a learner") is very different. While it may sometimes look like punishment, it isn't. Discipline is calm, intentional, planned. A younger father explains this word by showing how it works in his family with two children under three.

> *Discipline includes teaching good behavior, rewarding its emulation and punishing misbehavior. The "punishment" should be educational. But in some areas behavior can be extremely dangerous resulting in loss of life or limb. In these cases punishment serves as surrogate consequence. Children should*

learn from their mistakes before they are too consequential. They don't learn from fatal mistakes!

What a professor! While ready to use abrupt corrective techniques, if needed, he has a very clear picture of when they might apply, and why. Dangerous conditions are seen as needing different treatment in their school. No question. And good home-teachers use discriminating judgement in their classroom.

Still another young parent, a mother, isn't quite as sure of herself. As a result she comes at discipline a bit more hesitantly.

Discipline is a tough one. I'm never sure I'm doing it right. As soon as Jenny was able to walk and get into things she shouldn't, she was able to understand my no and obey it. But there came a time around age 1 when she began taking great joy in misbehaving. The more I tried to control her or chastise her the more she giggled—until I was ready to explode and she was nearly convulsed with laughter and delight. I felt as though I was seeing the Garden of Eden re-enacted in my own living room: The knowledge of good and evil in the form of a brand new concept that disobedience was within her power. No consequence could override the joy this power brought. Now that disobedience is old hat, things are a bit easier. The "time-

out" method works wonders, and when our requests are reasonable, she is usually perfectly happy to obey.

One more comment about discipline from the home-school front lines, echoed by many others.

I think discipline starts when a baby becomes mobile. It begins as the result of safety concerns about fire or falling or sharp things. It then broadens into general education about eating, care of self, getting along. But the same safety issue is a concern later: Be careful with gas and electricity, don't talk to strangers, be home before dark.

Effective parents have so much to share about the place of discipline in teaching. From the many comments about discipline in the school-in-our-home I excerpted this mosaic of 10 accents.

- *A key ingredient of family is discipline. Firm, loving, and consistent discipline is a must, and we are not afraid to "use the rod" when we must. Children have a right to know what their parents expect of them and what the consequences will be if they disobey.*

- *We set limits on the children in areas such as bedtime, types of snacks, punishment for disobeying. It is important that parents enforce their rules. That is hard at times. There are days when we wear* down easier. But they look for limits. They test us. If one does something wrong they sometimes let us know and then ask us if we aren't going to make them sit on the chair for 15 minutes.

- My folks were strict and consistent but never severe in punishment. I was spanked, but I was never spanked in anger or in front of friends or any other people. I always got a cuddle afterwards. Dad would say the usual, "This hurts me more than it hurts you." I couldn't see how that could be until I needed to spank my own children.

- Helen and I work at being consistent in our discipline. Most often we agree on behaviors that will cause us to discipline and decide together the form of discipline we will use.

- As far as disciplining the children is concerned, I would classify us as patient parents. Recently, my father was in town and told me he admired the patience I had with my son. He said he didn't think he could be that patient. I said, "I know. I remember." He laughed.

- Generally we give the kids freedom as long as the basic rules are followed. They are seldom punished by our denying anything. We often let correction come via natural consequences.

- When it comes to punishment, we have a couple of principles. One: Don't make a big deal out of unimportant issues. Nikki wanted a hair style in which one side of the head was shaved up to above her ears. We did not stop her. Later she decided not to do that again. She made the decision herself. And that leads to two: Let them make decisions as soon as they can on matters they can handle. If the consequences are traumatic, we help them. In this way, when they reach an age when more important decisions are needed, they know how to make them.

- Don't discipline a child when you are angry. You are apt to take out your hostilities on the child.

- The most important aspect of discipline is consistency. If one does not follow through on one's decisions, the child will never know what to expect from the parent.

- When Annie was about eight, she had trouble with lying. No amount of talk got through to her about how it hurt others and destroyed their trust in her. We decided to discipline. Her dad told her he would take her out for ice cream later. The *time came and she was ready, excited to go. He took her into her room and told her he had told her a lie and he was not going to take her out. She was crushed. But it made an impression. The lying stopped.*

In Wisconsin I came upon a great discipliner (remember, discipline means "to teach"). Within their school-in-our-home lived a daughter who was given to storming to her room and slamming the door behind her when she was displeased. Corrective admonition didn't have any effect. After one "storm" the father followed his daughter to her room where he, with no comment, took her door off its hinges and carried it to the basement. Two weeks later the door was replaced, again with no comment. Since then, it has only been slammed by unexpected gusts of summer wind. A lesson was taught—and learned. That's what schools are for.

Toward the end of letters, little pearls are sometimes discovered. Here's one.

We have learned as parents that it is important to increase our tolerance and lower our expectations.

Imagine the peace that sentence brings to their school-in-our-home!

I also appreciate this parent-teacher's off-handed report:

I have always been a bit nosey about what is going on in the children's lives and so has my husband. We ask a lot of questions even if it becomes annoying.

Educationally that sounds right on target.

Another insightful parent remembered:

Several years ago a teacher who had earlier taught each of our children remarked, "They are all good students, but each is so different from the other." I took that as a real compliment because it meant I allowed each of them to be themselves.

That is what the school-in-your-home is intended to produce. Children are different. Each needs to grow in different ways according to the blessings and gifts with which God has endowed them. Parents who understand that are good teachers.

Two last "gifts" for all who consciously teach in a school-at-home. These gifts come from effective parents. The first comes from Texas:

I have found, over and over again, that one can never say never about child-rearing rules. I have broken rules and changed my mind with each of our children. I am sure I will have to change more as our children grow.

And the last from a Kansas mother:

One key to making a family work is realizing the miracle of birth and grasping the tremendous responsibility of nurturing life. It's time-consuming—and you have to give it time. It's worrisome—and you have to be concerned. It's your responsibility—and you have to be involved. Doing these things will sometimes hurt, but you must make the sacrifice. I think that's one thing wrong with parents today. They won't make the sacrifice and in so doing fail to teach.

So what does the preceding chapter mean to a young parent who is not only reading about what others have done but who is working on her or his own skills? I tested it with a number of them. They offered four insights. Test them and maybe add a fifth.

First, they all concluded that teaching is not easy. That's almost Lesson 1 of developing a school-in-our-home. If it was easy, everyone would be doing it well. Quite clearly everyone *isn't* teaching well. So teaching calls for effort—intentional, vigorous effort.

Second, teaching in the home is a team effort. It's an application of Adam's view of Eve: "This is now bone of my bones and flesh of my flesh" (Gen. 2:23). He might just as well have added, " ... and teacher together with me." Even when there is no marriage partner, the best teaching still needs help via a friend, a parent, a relative, or someone in the community. It's not good to be alone.

Third, good teaching operates with clear standards. And with sensible and enforceable rules about the standards. And discipline to help students adhere to the standards.

Finally, the teaching process begins at birth and is shaped from the very start by the attitude of the parents. Parents who see themselves as educators are ready to make the most of all the teachable moments that surface in the school-in-our-home.

So where to go from here? Not far. We move from teaching as a commitment to how teaching happens. It happens in and through communication. That's next.

I'm Listening—
What Did You Say?

Our family has grown in awareness of the hurts of others. We try to listen instead of talk, do instead of offer, comprehend instead of criticize. Many in the family carry heavy burdens.

—An Iowa Father

We try to talk about everything as often as possible. Since we always seem to be on the go, it becomes difficult at times.

—A Washington Mother

We talk to her in English. She does not understand. But by pointing and making sounds we get her to understand our intentions. She does understand her name.

—An Illinois Mother of a 10-Month-Old

Don't try to tell young parents that they can't communicate with their wee ones—children under four years of age—or four months for that matter. They won't agree. They communicate with their children. Even the smallest. Even with their new-borns!

A mother of four, the oldest not yet 10, writes:

Having had four babies and nursing each for about six months, I can't imagine anyone ever doubting that a newborn communicates.

The father of a seven-month-old adds,

We talk to him. At seven months we know he cannot understand our words, but he knows what we say by the tone of our voice. We sometimes hear him say something that sounds like "Mom."

From the mother of a 2-½-year-old comes this insight into the communication process:

I communicate with John. I always answer his questions even if he doesn't understand the answer. We always listen when he talks and try never to divide our attention between him and things going on around us. We read to him daily. Communication is very important to us all.

Communication happens!

Who takes the lead in this communication process? And how? A Colorado mother, a little further down life's road, paints a broad-brushed picture of the dynamics of communication, one that is the same at every age:

*We try to explain to the children why we say yes or no to different requests. They seem to accept our answers better if we explain why we decided as we did. We don't say an automatic no. We are open and listen to what the person is saying—or listen for what they are **not** saying. Parents need to go back to their childhood and remember how they felt when they were that age. I follow my gut feelings if I don't feel comfortable with something or someone—or I avoid that subject all together. We talk about learning from someone else's mistakes. What led to the mistake? How would we have handled that problem? We talk about newspaper articles and letters to Ann Landers.*

How's that for a packed paragraph?

So what are we going to discuss in this chapter? Communication? Yes, but with a distinct accent. Read the Colorado mother's comments again. Woven into those sentences is the subject that effective parents identify as one of the most important aspects of communication there is— regardless of age. Correct and clear speech? No, not really. The other: listening.

Before we pinpoint that peak communication concern, listening, let's come at the bigger picture a little slower—and a step at a time. First of all, effective parents want us to know that the communication process is not automatic. Good communication demands conscious effort. It requires conscious effort from everyone in the family.

> *Open and honest communication is an important part of our family. I have my time with the girls when they arrive home from school. Their dad often takes walks with them in the evenings or on weekends. Occasionally we have three-hour dinner discussions.*

So writes an Indiana mother. Within those sentences is her own decision about the importance of communication, then that of her spouse. Both create times and opportunities for communication to happen. Next? They followed through. Without the action, what difference would a decision to communicate make?

Decisions to communicate—decisions, mind you—are the reason communication happens. Many effective parents noted that they had decided to communicate long before there were any children. The commitment to communicate was a building block of their marriage. One great couple decided:

> *A good marriage is the result of work and communication. You can't just get married and expect the euphoria of "until death do you part" to carry you through. We remembered the promise and then we worked and talked through difficult times.*

Worked and talked. Both.

So that's where communication starts. It starts with a decision to do it. It's hit-and-miss until that decision has been made. And if the decision has not been made between husband and wife, how likely is it to happen between parent and child? We move on.

Effective parents make pointed comments about the setting where communication happens best. One parent's view:

*Communication is something that Greg and I strive for with our children as well as with each other. Our goal is that our children will always feel comfortable coming to us with their problems. A house rule is no TV during supper. This is a **family** time. It is for sharing the day's activities. We feel it is important that each of us be aware of what is going on with the other family members.*

The same perspective from 2,000 miles away:

We eat supper together unless someone is at work. This is an established routine even if supper is simple. At mealtime I try to remind them of things that are coming up so they can fit them into their schedule. I also nag about what needs to be taken care of for school, church, etc. We try to be frank about finances, responsibilities, and other family concerns. No TV.

The no-TV-at-meals has been adopted by family after family. They say that since there is no better place to communicate than where the family gathers to eat, distractions are identified—and disallowed. With TV, effective parents see it as something much more than an annoyance. It is an enemy. Why? It powerfully blocks intra-family communication. They stop it. You can too. All it takes is a decision to put TV in its place.

Do younger parents see this? Oh yes.

TV can be our enemy. So writes one.

I'm not sure how TV fits into our life best. There is a temptation to let it be an electronic baby-sitter. I'm not sure that's all bad. But I also let it mind the baby when I'm right there—only I have something else I want to do rather than focus on the child. So writes another.

You may argue whether TV is enemy or friend, but this much is sure: If you or your child is concentrating on TV, you aren't listening to each other. That's what makes TV such a communication burden. It frustrates speaking. It frustrates hearing. A dad agrees:

When I want to listen or talk, I turn it off.

Lest you misunderstand the feelings about TV, parents aren't the only ones with anti-TV feelings. A Florida teen advises his peers:

Spend more time with your parents than watching TV, being on the telephone, or listening to your Walkman. Fewer lectures

result when they have your undivided atten-
tion.

Any questions?

A few years ago I wrote a book, "Let's Talk" (CPH, 1986), about the how of family communication. As the years pass, I have discovered that the feelings of parents and teens, which stirred that book to life, haven't changed. In 1986, I reported on a 1980 study that "over and over indicated parents and youth needing and wanting to communicate with each other. Both parents and youth want a happy family life, want to share values and information, want to talk." Nothing has changed on the home front since that report was written. Nothing. As a matter of fact, 1990 studies reveal the same feelings.

Since the problem hasn't changed, has the solution? Not really. The first step is still making a decision to act. And the decision? What would it look like? Now it's time to backtrack to where we were a few pages ago. The answer is that the decision is to listen. Listen.

A smart Maryland mother writes:

I've noticed that as the children have gotten older, my attention to them after school or in the evening has become even more important. I'll often start with an innocent question such as, "What did you eat for lunch today?" or "Who did you eat with?" I may ask about what happened in a particular

class and soon they are telling me all sorts
of things, good and bad. They've even said,
"Why am I telling you this?" But they don't
stop talking. Sarah's friends have told her,
"You tell your parents everything!"

There's a smart, effective mother, accomplished in the art of communication. She listens.

How many repeats of the communicate-by-first-listening insight would you like? Five? No problem. More, if you wish.

- *Mom and Dad made each of us feel special. All four of us kids were very different and each had certain areas where we excelled. My parents watched, listened, and always found something positive to comment upon.*

- A father who inherited a ready-made family later in his life wrote: *After being single for so long I had to learn to be there for them when I might have wanted to be elsewhere. I listen to what is important to them even when I have other things on my mind.*

- Another dad tells us: *God has blessed us with seven-year-old Daniel and five-year-old Rebecca. In many ways they are often the teachers and we are the students. How refreshing it is to hear their view of life and how they perceive it! We listen to our children and let them tell us their sides of the story. My wife and I recall that as children, our parent's word was law and we were not allowed to respond. By listening we have learned the importance of apologizing when the situation calls for it. Our children understand that we, as parents, make mistakes and are not infallible.*

- From mom's perspective: *Listening is essential to our family. My husband is great at that, working things through before giving advice. Usually they take his advise. Harping does not help.*

- Do single parents know this too? *To compensate for the lack of a two-parent family, my daughter and I have always treated our time together as quality family time. We listen to each other. Listening is the key.*

And how does this fit the youngest parents? Watch what happens in your life. Does your child tug at your trousers saying, "Daddy ... Daddy ... Daddy" without a let up? Or "Mama ... Mama ... Mama"? That's a call for listening. Of course, many of those earliest calls are inconsequential. Who cares that "Bobby stuck his tongue out at me?" But what a parent does care about is that a process of speaking/listening is established. Early. Those incidental calls for listening become prime moments for talking about communication, for teaching that messages ought to have some worth to both, for demonstrating focused care. It starts as soon as they can talk.

But even before that, the speaking/listening process is in place as the parent talks and coos and looks into the baby's eyes and responds to every primal communication effort. It teaches the baby that you care. It teaches you how to listen.

There you have it. They all say the same thing: Listening is at the heart of communication. Not half-hearted listening. There's even a name for the kind of listening that's needed. It's called **active listening**.

Active listening is more than concentrated listening. Active listening is a hearing that is followed by feedback. That feedback must let the sender know you have received his or her message.

Suppose your child said, "Mom, I'm hungry." Instead of an absent-minded acknowledgement, an active listener might reply, "It sounds to me like you didn't have enough at lunch—a big guy like you needs lots of food." It also may be the chance to open a discussion on the time supper ought to be served, when Dad is coming home, or how much energy it takes to climb trees. You can open the door to a dozen different subjects with his opening, if you are into active listening. Active listening does not assume. It probes and shares and listens and responds and builds relationships.

A Texas mom supports the process of active listening without calling it by that name when she urges:

Listen to each other. But don't just silently receive what is said. React.

Her "sister" in Minnesota agrees, adding:

Try to understand where the child is coming from. Listen carefully. They may not be saying what they are feeling. Reword their comments to make sure they mean what you think they mean.

Both are actually encouraging active listening.

Active listening not only tests your accuracy of perception, it also fills in the conversational lulls that develop when someone is not sure what to say next. Classes that teach active listening are regularly offered through community schools, at churches, even from family service agencies. The name by which it is known is not always the same, but the end product is. When all is said and done, you hear better, which in turn puts your responses right on target.

All this accent on listening is not intended to say that clarity of speech is unimportant. Quite the contrary. It is very important. The spoken/written word is a basic medium for sharing feelings, passing on information, or giving advice. That's why I was surprised effective parents didn't say much about the importance of clear speech. That void troubled me. I was so perturbed that I went back through my letters, notes, comments, and interviews seeking an answer. And I found it. The first clue came from interviews with the younger parents. One said:

> *Why would you accent talking? We do that all the time. It's assumed that speaking is a key element of communicating.* What's not assumed is that listening is too.

There you have it: Little is said about the importance of clear speech because it is assumed. It is a given. Effective parents do not have much to say about givens. They focus on what's missing in the communication equation. When it comes to communicating, listening is the most common missing link.

But there is more in the communication mix that concerns effective parents. Specifically, effective parents worry about three bad guys: double-messages, you-messages, and incomplete-data-messages.

A double-message is a message that can easily be interpreted in more than one way. When Dad answers a little tyke's request to visit the zoo on Saturday with, "Maybe," that's a double message. Does he mean maybe-yes or maybe-no? The same goes for "Later" or "Sometime." Those are all double messages. They don't bring peace and wholeness to a family. They set the stage for the pain of unrealized expectations. They are so unnecessary. Jesus can help you here. He said once, "Simply let your 'Yes' be 'Yes,' and your 'No,' be 'No'" (Matt. 5:37). That's very appropriate in family communication, particularly as you deal with the youngest ones. They take your words seriously.

And the you-message? Another bad guy. A you-message is accusatory. It dumps on the recipient. It puts listeners on the spot, making them feel like they are in a court of law standing before a judge. You-messages are loaded with words like "always" or "never" as in "You always leave the door open" and "You never pick up your toys." You-messages have sharp teeth that rip and shred. They attack. Don't use a you-message unless you mean to. Even then, reserve you-messages for the few times they might do some good. Never waste one on piffle.

Incomplete-data-messages complete the treacherous trio. An incomplete-data-message is when you ask that something be done but don't give the supporting information that would tell how, and when, and why. It's like instructing your child to empty a waste basket without saying which one—or which ones. Unless you tell them, they don't know whether you meant the basket in the bathroom or under the kitchen sink. And they don't yet know whether you mean right now, or before supper, or by the weekend. All that may be known to you, but not to your child.

So what can you do about these three enemies of good communication? First, recognize they exist and that they are dangerous.

Second, realize that the responsibility for the clearer spoken word is with the speaker. Who else? One mom summarizes all this, saying:

We feel it is important to talk, talk, talk. Nothing is resolved by running off to a room and shutting the door. Even if tempers run high, we agree to talk, but we may wait a while before we do. Then we talk about how we feel. No personal attacks or insults are allowed.

I love that quote. She says: No double-messages; no you-messages; no incomplete-data-messages. If those three nasties were controlled, the communication process would improve 100%. Automatically! Add in careful listening, active listening, and clear speech, and the change would be 1,000%.

There's yet another area of communication sensitivity that should concern us. It was not spelled out, as such, in the effective parents' comments about communication. It showed up elsewhere, and this book places it in the chapters dealing with love, with touching, and with forgiveness. This special communication concern has to do with how an effective parent corrects, admonishes, or sends a negative message to a son or daughter. In those moments the packaging is everything.

Negative, or corrective, messages are best sent with sender and receiver close enough to each other that they can hold hands (now there's an idea!), look into the other's face, and speak quietly. All that. Then, maybe, if all three conditions are maintained, not only the words but the feelings will also get through. Who wins if a parent later appeals, "How could she have taken it *that* way?" The more sensitive the issue *to the receiver* the greater care ought be taken by the sender with the message.

One more area of potential communication confusion: humor. Humor will be dealt with as a separate and important subject in a later chapter. Here it is mentioned as important because it can easily be misunderstood.

Not everything is humorous to everyone, as a wife who makes this observation about her husband, knows. She writes:

Another thing I feel is important is communication. This has to be the hardest thing we have to deal with in our family. If we could trust each other enough to know that we don't mean to be offensive, it might be different. Leon is and has always been a character. I'm very sensitive to the needs and feelings of others and I'm often offended by my husband's sense of humor. But, thank God, through experience and learning to communicate with him, I've learned to understand what a fun-loving man he really is. I now accept him and do not try to change him. That is important.

Humor, as a method of communication, depends on so many variables. If the subject is important, don't try to wrap it in humor unless you are very sure how it is being received.

Be careful how you talk about the littlest ones when they are present. Cute stories about your kids probably shouldn't get past the two parents—maybe with a grandparent or two thrown in. And if the story is shared more broadly, it should not be told when the child is present, or in such a way that the child is the object of ridicule, or if he/she is likely to be approached about the matter by another. No story is worth the embarrassment that even the youngest feel. You can tell when they are hurt or ashamed or flustered. Don't do that to your child. One young mother wisely said:

We don't make fun of our children.

Communication that blossoms in listening and speaking is not the only essential element of effective parenting. There's another touching subject. It is just that—a touching subject. See what effective parents will make of that lead.

A Touching Subject

People were bringing little children to Jesus to have Him touch them. ... He took the children in His arms, put His hands on them and blessed them."

—Mark 10:13, 16

When my father didn't touch me, I didn't know if he cared. There is a communication void that is filled with miscommunication, misconception, and wrong ideas when nothing is done about touching. When my father hugged me, I knew I was his son and nothing that I would ever do could change that. It's not enough to say you love or care for someone. The action must be there as well.

—A Texas Son Remembers

We touch, smell, and hug each other so that when we are separated we can vividly recall our times together.

—An Illinois Mother

Touching? A chapter on touching? Whose idea is that? Effective parents, that's who. They insist that touching is important and they tie it to how they think effective parents show love and display affection in their family. To think: Our middle class effective Christian parents are committed to touching! It was only after I reflected on my own life practices that touching began to make sense. I, too, am a toucher.

As a pastor I touch people. I touch the foreheads of babies I baptize and young people I confirm. I touch pastors with the laying on of my hands at their ordinations. When I pray with the sick or the troubled, I take their hand. Standing at death's door with a member in a hospital's intensive care ward, we touch. The prayers at our breakfast/lunch/dinner table never feel better than when our family joins hands. And, yes, my grandchildren like to hang onto one of my fingers when we walk. They like to do so as much as their moms and dads did when they were little ones. Looking back I recall with pleasure those glorious courting days when Audrey and I were such great hand holders. We still are. As I think of it, we really touched a lot in the Kansas home of my youth. I can't remember anyone teaching me to touch—or talking about it as important. We just did it. So why the silence in our world today about something that was such an important part of life in the past, and still is important today?

Could the reason we talk so little about touching be that touching is not only an age-old expression of love but that it also has a dark side? A side stained by sin? It does. Molesters touch. Murderers and sexual deviates too. And what's the line about the crook "who always has his hand in your pocket?" I wonder if the fear of having our touching actions confused with the clutching of one of those makes us all hesitant to evaluate and discuss touching in a much more open and honest fashion.

Whatever—I was never specifically taught much about touching. Yet, taught—or not—I did it. And I still do. Effective parents do too. It's probably the reinforcement I receive that makes me so appreciative of the way effective parents speak about touching. What's nice is that they are joined in their support of touching by some very touching people: (1) Dr. Gary Chapman, a well-known Christian pastor, writer, teacher, and counselor from North Carolina, (2) Jesus Christ, and (3) the young moms and dads who filled out questionnaires I sent them.

I'll begin with Dr. Chapman because he first alerted me to the wondrous relationship between love and touching. In so doing he sensitized me to the power in touching. All that happened when I heard an audiotape in which he asserted that everyone expresses love in at least one (maybe more!) of five ways: through gifts, by acts of kindness, with words, in quality time, and—you guessed it—via touch.

In support of his position Dr. Chapman showed how Jesus used every one of these expressions of love at some time in His life and ministry. After this claim I reread Matthew, Mark, Luke, and John looking for instances of Jesus showing love in ways that matched Dr. Chapman's sequence. The examples were easy to find, especially touch. When He isn't touching people, they are touching Him. Look for yourself. Touching is a very Christ-like—and Christian—thing. It actually visualizes that hard-to-define word, love.

When Dr. Chapman develops his insight into the five expressions of love, he makes two additional observations that I find fascinating: (1) Everyone uses one of the five cited expressions as their primary demonstration of love and (2) people feel most loved when another responds to them using the same expression as do they. Think about that!

An additional fascination about Dr. Chapman's list is that another of his five-star expressions will be featured by effective parents in a later chapter. Can you guess which? I'll tell you. It's the other T-word: time.

I realize I've spread Dr. Chapman's love-net wider than the specific subject of this chapter would seem to require, but I've done so for a reason. I shared with you all five expressions of love so that you could see how touching fits so perfectly in among them. Touching, our specific subject, fits right in among those other bold and bright expressions of love. In that context touch still shines.

Effective parents believe it shines—actually blazes. They believe that the touch of love has power. An effective parent who is also a nurse opens her letter with: *"Love for Christ is the cornerstone of family."* We've certainly made that point already, right? She continues:

After that comes love for one's self and for each other. Touching is important in my profession as a nurse. I have tried to make it an important part of my family as well. A loving touch, whether it be a hug, a tap on the arm, or even sitting close, can let others know how much they mean to you.

As far as this nurse/mother is concerned, her touch is visible love full of energy. Does anyone agree with her? Many.

From Ohio an effective dad wants us to know:

It's important for children to see that their parents are affectionate. We hug a lot. Our children do too.

A Kansas dad encourages us *to show kids love in many ways—hugs, words, special treats, notes in their lunch. It's also important that Mom and Dad show love for each other.*

A Texas parent adds: *We are a very affectionate family. Hugging, kissing, and snuggling are important to all of us, even our 11-year-old son. There are times Mom shouldn't hold his hand, but at home he still loves affection.*

From Washington, a mother says:

We are physically affectionate as a family. We hold hands, hug, walk arm in arm, sit close while we read the paper, hold hands when we pray, and never meet after being apart without some affectionate display.

Lastly, from North Carolina, an effective parent, who is also a teacher, gives touching an educational dimension.

I am discouraged by the lack of love shown to children in many families. So many seem neglected. Touch is very important. Too many children are not personally touched and lovingly touched in families any more. Husbands and wives should never be ashamed to hug each other in front of family. Hug the kids. If they feel they are too old to be hugged, touch them in other ways. Physical touch does so much.

Effective moms and dads are determined that touching, as an expression of love, must not die with them. A resolute southern mom puts it this way:

We learned through the years that physical expressions of love are important. At 12 or 13, our youngest pulled away from a hug and a kiss and was told in no uncertain

terms he would never be too old for kisses.
He was astonished to be told that. He never
pulled away again. We feel his teen years
were easier because of our physical close-
ness and inner warmth. Our older children
had gone through the same kind of with-
drawal, which we at first permitted, until
we realized that kisses and hugs helped us
all.

Having come out strong for touching, a number of effective parents were quite specific about
their times of touching and the methods they use.
One mom said:

Playing with kids and touching them makes
for bonding. A real kinship or feeling of
"buddies" develops. Oh, the parent/child
relationship is still maintained, but a differ-
ent closeness results.

From another, this report of evening closeness, variations of which were reported again and
again:

The final part of the bedtime routine is a
hug, a kiss, and an I-love-you. All that
builds security and lets them know that, no
matter what happened during the day, our
love for them as a unique person is unwa-
vering. At the same time we model God's
unconditional love for them too.

Interested in something unique in the world
of touch? At least it seemed unique to me—until

it showed up in families unknown to each other and miles removed. For the moment one will report for both.

I'm not sure who started it but we have in our family what we call a "group hug." Any member of the family is free to ask for a "group hug" at any time for any reason. We then all hug each other simultaneously. We do it because it gives us a good feeling and it's a way to show our love for each other.

After that outpouring from effective parents about touching, hugging, and kissing, I decided to probe the moms and dads of the littlest ones on this subject. I asked them, very directly, "What's the place of touching/holding/hugging in your relationship with your baby?" Did they answer? Did they ever! Following are a few of the responses from younger parents. I see them as the up-to-the-minute report of touching, in our time.

- *We hug and cuddle and rough house a lot.*

- *Touching is very important. Rachel climbs over us and we have a three-way hug with her sandwiched between us. Study after study has shown the importance of touching for babies—and for the health of us all.*

- *We hug and pick up the baby more and more as she grows older. On an airplane ride when she was four months old, she looked at me and seemed to be scared as the plane was taking off. I smiled at her, held her hand, and told her it was okay, at which point she smiled and relaxed. The rest of the plane ride she was a perfect baby.*

- *Physical contact is very important. In fact we give great big hugs and kisses for going to the potty rather than candy and stickers. We do a lot of hugging and kissing. It comes naturally. I was raised by an Italian mother!*

Italian mother? Nationality means nothing. That punch line is the same whether you were raised by a Swedish, German, Japanese, or Brazilian mother! Add your own country of origin too. Hugging is international!

- *Hugging, holding, and touching are important ways to communicate love and caring for your child. I make sure to include all three in our daily lives. It's important for the child as well as the adult.* Note all those for whom this exercise is important: (1) the child and (2) the adult.

- *Physical affection is a very key part of our relationship with Eric. It demonstrates in a real way how we feel about him. One thing we started early with Eric, that now he loves and asks for all the time, is the "family hug." That's a great moment for*

Mom, Dad, and Eric. As mentioned, this family isn't related to the family-huggers of a few paragraphs back. They live half a country apart.

- *Hugging, touching, and holding are how you spend your time with a baby. Each child responds differently.*

- *Physical contact with the baby and the three-year-old is important. It is calming and reassuring. It's a silent way to confirm your love and acceptance.*

- *Hugging is what we do, consistently, the major part of our day.*

There were more great comments, each with a little different insight, or offering a tiny but important twist. Still the message was the same: Touching is important. I should have known they would say that, especially since all my life I've heard tender and emotional scenes described as "touching moments." Am I dense! But no longer. My eyes are open. I am done with understating the place and power of touch. It is crucial to effectiveness not only for parenting but in life itself.

If you want to further test the thesis of this chapter, dig around in the Old Testament for all the touching, holding, embracing, and physical contact between those who love and care for each other. The touch is unbelievably important. But, then, so is the subject of the next chapter. We shift from the touch in "touching moments" to the other half of that expression: the moments. Mound those moments and they become minutes and hours and days: time. It's time to talk about time.

Time and Time—Again

I try to put a priority on family time. Not just quality time (a favorite phrase for families who don't spend much time with their kids) but quantity time as well. I think small children spell love: T-I-M-E.

—A Michigan Father

We did things together as a family. I have many vivid memories of fun times when the kids were little. Every Sunday afternoon we went somewhere together—to the park to feed the ducks, to the zoo to ride the train, to the swimming pool. Most of the activities were inexpensive or free. We ate out every Sunday evening, even if it was McDonald's. I remember asking for two high chairs and a booster seat.

—A Texas Mother

Family is very important. Not just immediate family, but parents, grandparents, and cousins. Reunions have been a part of our life every year.

—A Colorado Mother

141

I read with fascination the findings of a recent University of Michigan study that asked the question, "Why have the children of recent Southeast Asian immigrants, of otherwise ordinary background, done so well in school?" The answer comes in two related parts.

First, those kids do homework. They do it every day. They do two to three times as much homework as their American-born classmates in the United States. That makes a difference. Second, they do their homework *as a family*. That really makes a difference.

The University of Michigan report says it works this way: "Homework is the focus of Asian refugee family life on weeknights. The whole family gathers around the table, working together. Older children typically help younger siblings. Even when parents cannot help directly with assignments because of limited English, they stress the importance of study and see to it that no family chores interfere with study. Children whose parents read to them regularly, either in English or in their native language, do better in school than others. Regardless of their language skills those parents pass on shared wisdom, cultural values, and emotional closeness."

Summary? They give each other *the* most precious gift one family member can give another. It's the gift that is the heart of every other gift. They give each other time. Best of all, their gift is *family* time.

That word, time, encapsulated one of the most intense themes that threaded through the letters and interviews of effective moms and dads. The younger parents were, if anything, even more earnest in their beliefs about time. Both groups of parents were in full agreement on the importance of time. But *real* time—no fakey imitation time. They believe in 60-seconds-a-minute time with no provisos, caveats, weasely definitions, or evasions. One younger dad, actually speaking for all the parents who responded, wants us to know:

> *"Quality time" is a farce. When it comes to time spent with your children, there can be no quality without quantity. The more children you have, the more time you should invest in them. It is important to spend time together as a group and also time with each child.*

Sounds like he's from one of those Southeast Asian families!

But that's not the whole of what effective parents have to say about time. Here are four time-ly comments from effective parents:

- *It takes a lot of time and energy to support a child. Not all parents take the time mine did—and still do to this day.*

- *Recently my son John, age 8, asked me, out of the blue, "Dad, do you know why I like you so much?" I didn't try to answer. "Because you spend time with us kids."*

- *The girls know, not because we tell them but because of where we spend our time, that the important things in our lives are our church, our faith, our family, and education. We plan our lives around our priorities.*

- *It takes time to do family. Lots of it. As a teacher I see daily evidence of parents who do not take time to do family.*

Effective parents, and their families, are committed to spending time with each other. Get it clear: They hoot at all who try to talk about quality time and quantity time as if they were two sides of the same coin and that you are free to chose one or the other for your family. In effective families there is no such thing as quality time that is not also quantity time. Period. There can be quantity time that is not quality time, sad to say. But never the reverse.

Okay, so effective families spend time with each other. What do they do that makes their time expenditure so important?

They do a lot of things with their time. But, strange to say, they do not do a lot of different things. That's true whether the parents are old hands at parenting or brand new. Actually their time falls into a few broad categories.

One key category, one that has come up in some way in every chapter of this book, doesn't even look like it ought to be seen as family time. An Illinois husband says:

> *Marge and I, as parents, know we have to take time for ourselves and for each other. It's difficult to give from an empty pocket.*

The remarkable part of that quote is that when they take time for themselves as parents, they do so as a conscious part of their strategy for building family. Determined to remain effective, husbands and wives identify the time they spend with each other as being at the heart of family building.

They are not alone in their conclusion. A Maryland mom says of herself and her husband:

> *Every night, right after dinner, we go into our room for 30 minutes to an hour of private adult talk. The children understand that we are not to be disturbed unless really necessary. After this time together we devote the remainder of the evening to the children and their needs. We both feel that our relationship is the foundation of the family and therefore it needs to be healthy and strong.*

Think back through all the sections we have covered. How many times is the care and nurture of the marriage identified as crucial to the health of the family! When the marriage is in trouble, the family is in trouble because it's the marriage that God uses to bring order to the home. Could that be why Paul speaks as plainly about marriage as he does in Ephesians 5? His words there, and elsewhere, make me sure that he was a family man. He would join his modern successors at marking up time with your parent-partners as a high priority use of parental time. But, remember, that's time with your partner—not just a couple hours hanging around the same area where he or she is. That's the first point effective parents make about family time. But there is more.

Many letters emphasize using time for building family traditions.

> A tradition that takes time for us is a celebration after report cards. We don't require that our children achieve a grade average—just that the child works hard and tries to do his or her best. We find something positive and we take time to celebrate it, says a Louisiana mother.

A Wisconsin family has its time that is related to traditions too.

> In our family we have developed daily routines and traditions which encourage conversation and time together. On a daily basis we eat breakfast and supper together. This is done at a table without TV or radio distractions. Of course, every rule has its exception. Ours is Green Bay Packers and Wisconsin Badger games. Otherwise mealtime is an

opportunity for family members to share their day's plans and experiences.

I like that: a tradition within a tradition. Timely traditions, both, that also demonstrate how renegotiation can and should fit into the family. Sometime!

Two more. One from Texas and the other from Minnesota.

Writes the one: *The past two years my uncles and cousins have come home for Christmas. It's a lot of work, especially for Mother, and it takes time. When they leave, we say we'll never do that again. But we will. Why? We have a tradition that started in the 1800s that on Christmas Eve we eat futchens for supper, sing carols, open gifts, and eat, eat, eat. I hope my children carry this on.*

The other is just as direct. *One goal I have is to instill a sense of tradition in my children. When I was young, my family traditionally took a family vacation in Florida. Some of my best memories are of all of us playing softball on the beach. We also, traditionally, went to church Christmas Eve and opened presents Christmas morning. We had many peculiarities and rituals that every family has—all those year-after-year, you-can-count-on-it routines that make for a secure and stable household.*

Is any of that possible without saving up and then intentionally using time?

An Oregon mother doesn't call what she is doing building traditions. For her it's simpler than all that. She says,

We strive to make our own family memories.

Any of us could do that. All it takes is time.

And where else do families chose to allocate big wads of time? Vacations:

We live for our vacations and we take them as a family.

How direct can you get? I'll reinforce that simple sentence with two expansions.

- *Try to set aside some vacation time together. It may only be a long weekend or an extended two-week vacation. We always vacationed with Grandma, Grandpa, Lilah, and me. Grandpa is now gone. But I still make sure that Grandma, Lilah, and I take time to get away for long weekends or two weeks together. It bonds us as a family.*

- *Family vacations are another priority with us. Being together for a vacation is an opportunity to teach your children your love of nature, your favorite hobby, your interest in history, or your desire to learn something new.*

There's one more insight into the subject of time and vacationing that needs hearing:

We don't believe in taking a vacation without our daughter. We will have plenty of time to do that alone when she gets out on her own.

This effective mother does not mean that she and her husband do not have dates and dinners without their daughter. They do. But vacations are different. In those instances time commitments are not made without everyone being involved.

Besides using their time to develop traditions and take vacations, what else do effective parents do with their time? One mother sets time aside to keep a diary.

I guess it has become therapy. When I am concerned or worried, I look back and remember a similar time and God's faithfulness is recorded. My worry was in vain— which I know is always true, but somehow I keep needing reminding.

A dad, who admits he doesn't talk as much as he would like, adds:

I show my love by supporting our children as much as possible by doing things such as delivering their papers when they had athletic practice (once the wind chill was 65° below zero, attending their games, band concerts, and plays almost to the point of never missing. And then discussing the joys and hurts afterwards.

Want to be as effective as that effective father? All it takes is a commitment to do what's needed—and a willingness to take the time.

Another father talks about the use of time this way:

Parents must take time to play with their kids—not occasionally, not on holidays only. Daily. Do it at the supper table, while taking a bath, at the playground, or walking with them. It's too easy for adults to never play with their kids. Let things go in order to regularly interact with your kids. Our neighbors have a beautiful lawn, a boat, the works. They maintain their home and their possessions. When they first put up their swing set, their two-year-old got on and just sat there. Neither parent had time to push. That seemed like torture to me.

A few more reports about time, its use—and the importance with which it is viewed:

- *I spend a lot of time with my children. We play basketball, baseball, swim, collect cards. My father was always working so we did not spend much time together. That is my worst memory of childhood. I cannot recall playing catch with my father.*

- *As the chief cook I serve meals at a time when people can be home and we have a relaxed time to eat. Sometimes we eat at 5 o'clock because of an evening meeting. Other times we eat at 8 o'clock because someone is getting home late from work or school. This requires flexibility and planning, but it shows the children that family members are valuable and we want to spend time with them.*

- *About the time our oldest son entered junior high, Rick gave up officiating high school basketball and football games so that we could have Friday night for family. We reasoned that if we attended sports events with them while they were young, we would be accepted as a fixture when they reached high school. It worked. But it took time.*

- *A daily routine that has worked well for our family is that we "put" each child to bed every night. We say our prayers and take time to talk about the day's activities on a one-to-one basis. At that time we really try to listen and avoid lecturing. For a while, when they were small, I would pray with the three of them together. But keeping track of whose room, whose bed, and who goes first wore me out and got in the way of the purpose of our time together. It takes longer now, but it's worth it.*

So now you know why I was overwhelmed by the intentional ways effective parents spend time with their children. Even more overwhelming to me is how much all that time totals. I am certain that effective parents in my survey spend as much time with their children as the Southeast Asian parents I referenced at the beginning of this chapter. A Florida mother supports my conviction saying, about their family:

Everyone supports each other in their individual endeavors, attending each other's concerts, sporting events, and the like. Evening meals are eaten together with devotions and reading done together after the meal. Time is also taken for family fun.

There is a careful side of the time question too. Effective parents repeatedly caution about how non-family time can intrude on family time. So writes an experienced and highly mobile father:

Through many moves we have discovered an important need for our family: Do not over commit. We realized we needed more time with each other, just for us. This allows for family trips, talking, better awareness of each other's needs. We make rules about how many clubs, sports events, and the like we can commit to. Parents too. It was hard establishing the idea at first, but everyone accepts it as routine now.

And what insights about time from our parents of young children? One caring mom says it all, for all:

A baby takes a tremendous amount of time —more hours than there are in a day. There's feeding, bathing, diapering, clothes changes, playtime, reading time, and comforting time. And even if you find time to do something else while your child's around, the child isn't likely to let you. They want your attention. Failing that they want to see what's so interesting to you and play with it themselves.

Babies take time. Tons of it.

So, young moms and dads, brace yourself. There's a world of time-consuming commitments just waiting your acceptance. I've wondered why there isn't a Candyland competition in the Olympics! If you're not sure what that sentence means, then you need more time with your little-older-little-ones. And how about reading—just plain reading. Books such as Dr. Seuss and "The Little Engine That Could." And great videos await your family viewing and your parental interpretation. "Pinocchio" and "Beauty and the Beast" are best seen at toddler times with Mom and Dad present. Questions? You can't believe the questions and the chances you have for cracking open doors of understanding. Or more.

Car games. Color identity games. Animal games. First efforts at ball games as those large muscles grow. Bicycle rides on a toddler's seat for the very young and and then riding bikes together when they get older. Time at the park for learning about safety—and taking turns. Walks, strolls, trots, runs, and ambles. All take time and all build togetherness. Rough-housing, laughing, learning how to lose, family building projects, gardens that guarantee a product. All those things and more poured out of the conversations with younger parents. It reminded me again that you need to be in shape to spend time with your sons and daughters.

The effective parents' understanding of time and their decisions about how it will be used clearly shape families—parent and child alike. I knew that. But I was unprepared for the vehemence with which effective families claim that sentence. And I was not at all aware how totally many (most?) commit themselves to the creative uses of time for family.

A representative Wisconsin father is the voice of many:

> *I feel we are a close family. I try to give my children what they need to have fun and enjoy life. We do things together: vacation, bike ride, hike. We joined the Milwaukee Brewer fan club and go to six or more*

Brewer games a year. I give myself to my family. I don't always do what I want, but what they want instead. We eat meals together. We go to church together. We communicate. Sherry and I help them with their homework.

So you better take time for time. If you wonder whether you do—keep track. Maintain a diary. Set a goal of how much family-building time you are willing to spend. Divide it between the parts and the whole, making sure each child (and your marriage partner too) get the gift of time from you. You'll never regret the time you spent with either. You'll grieve in later years for all the hours that got away. Establish the pattern when the children are tiny and let the product develop from there.

While time and its use are not laughing matters, there are lots of other things in life that are. Humor and laughter make family life sweet and soften many of life's sharper edges. Next chapter. More surprises.

Humor, Laughter, and Effectiveness

◆

Humor is so important. If I hadn't been able to laugh at some of the hardest times, I don't think I could have survived. To be able to laugh and go on when you want to cry and quit is a blessing. Don't get me wrong. There were times when I had a good cry.

—A Virginia Mother

One of the qualities I have always enjoyed in my husband is his sense of humor. I find that our laughing together not only makes our marriage and family life more fun but also helps to relieve the tension.

—An Oregon Mother

Humor—another subject I wasn't expecting. Who would have thought humor was critical to effective family living? No matter, effective families urge the inclusion of humor in the honor roll of positive family ingredients. Granted, there was no pressing urgency behind its inclusion. As a matter of fact the whole subject almost escaped me. I would have missed it entirely except my subconscious picked up on the persistent regularity with which it appeared. By count, it was one of the most mentioned topics, usually slipped in toward the end of a letter or conversation in a kind of oh-by-the-way fashion. On a 0 to 10 intensity-of-mention scale, humor/laughter/fun would probably be about a two, mentioned about as casually as this aside by a midwest mother:

It's important to keep a sense of humor.

So what's the big deal? If it's so important to keep a sense of humor why isn't it mentioned more emphatically? I would guess for the same reasons we don't say a lot about the importance of breathing, or eating, or exercise, or a lot of other things. It is assumed. And that's the first point. Family humor—like breathing, exercise, and eating—goes largely unmentioned and unnoticed in life. Until it is absent. Then its absence is noticed everywhere and affects everything.

Humor and laughter are just as important and much more in evidence within the families of the very young, with one difference. In the families of the young, the focus of the humor and laughter is of a more limited scope. The subject matter isn't very wide ranged. The subject is the baby. And it's usually further limited to the visual world of what-the-baby-did-today. Even within that category the focus tightens down even more to biological functions (I heard a hundred hilarious dirty diaper stories), outrageous conduct, embarrassing moments, and surprising reactions. Humor in the home with little ones is old-fashioned, highly visual low comedy.

By the time I collected anecdotes (and every family has dozens of stories that fit the category), a couple things became obvious. The antics are funniest if the child involved is your own. It's okay if the subject is the child of a friend or your cousin Ruth, but even then it's not the same as if it happened to your own little dumpling.

Another insight? After reading about a hundred funny things that happened with kids, then listening to a half-hundred more, I discovered that the humor did not lie with the child. The humor was latent within the adult and spotted by the adult as it erupted through the child. Humorless parents never had any funny stories to tell—not about their children, not about themselves. And they don't join in with laughter when others are giggling with glee. They nod. They acknowledge an event. They even repeat the punch line. ("Oh, yes, the baby fell into the toilet, right.") But there is no exuberant reaction. No good-natured recognition of the uproarious potential of the human race. Nope. Not with them. They just note an event and move on. Too bad for them—and their families.

While noting what I noted, I recognized that the range of humor in the home is much wider than the latest tricks of a much loved 12-month-old. Parents that laugh with and about their children also laugh with many other family members and friends about a wide range of subjects. They don't focus all their feelings about fun into a narrow segment of their family world. They find humor in all the corners of life and a way to laugh at all levels.

Here are a few illustrations of what I mean. I'll start with an humor-filled Illinois wife who wrote:

> *I prayed for a husband who liked baseball.* Any humor so far? Just wait. She continues: *Dick was on a minor league club with the Cubs when I met him* .... A little smile, maybe, that leads to a boffo ending, ... *so I knew he was God's chosen one for me.*

Can you imagine that last line being delivered to a room full of relaxed relatives at the 25th anniversary celebration of that couple's marriage? I can. Right this moment I can hear the laughter in her voice as she works her way to the punch line, her eyes dancing with anticipated delight, intentionally hesitating in her delivery. That's how I think she'd do it. But then I have an advantage. I read the rest of her letter. Line after line made me laugh as she reported home events, giving her life's experiences gentle twist after gentle twist. She's obviously fun to be around and knows how to keep your attention as she makes her points with good humor.

Her letter demonstrates two other important insights about humor and its use in home and family. The first is that if there is any possibility of embarrassment, family humorists always make themselves the object of the laughter. In family humor other persons who are part of the story are never presented in such a way that they are held up for ridicule or shame. If there's going to be laughter at someone's expense, it's always the teller of the tale who pays that price.

A second insight is that it's a lot funnier if you were there when the big event happened or if you know the frailties of all those who are part of the funny story. If neither of those conditions fit, the story's hilarity is easily lost—unless the teller can surprise you into a smile through the way a situation is presented. I'll let another "humorist" show what I mean. You may be surprised at where she found humor.

> *A sense of humor is a must in life. We've done a lot of teasing in our family and never realized how natural it was until we had foster kids who were never quite sure if we were serious. We laugh at serious times, too, especially when we need it most. Our 26-year-old Navy pilot son-in-law was lost at sea flying at night. Nothing was ever found of his plane. He left our daughter and two small children. As we waited during the search, young Navy wives came two at a time to pay respects and bring a meal. After crying together they would leave and we'd check to see what they brought for supper.*

Each must have changed the meal plan. We had chicken every day. When we told the gal who had organized the setup, she informed us that her daughter had broken out in chicken pox that day. All this gave us laughter with our tears.

A similar letter was from a lady who had gone to her father's funeral in a city two states away. People brought food to her mother's house where the grieving family was gathered. That family dealt with its grief by "rating" all the food offerings. They even gave wry awards! When she returned home, she explained all this to her husband who had not been able to attend with her. He didn't think it was at all funny. The last line of her letter? *I guess you had to be there.* Yes, and have a sense of not only what that family was feeling but how it uses humor to deal with grief.

As unembellished anecdotes, those last two stories aren't all that humorous. Right? But they are, especially to the families involved. At the root of the humor is the Christian truth that they chose to confront death, the enemy Christ overcame on the cross, with laughter—as well as tears. Their low-keyed "ha-ha" echoes Paul's 1 Corinthians 15 statement of faith. Please note, too, that the lead laughers in the two stories are not giddy children. They are mature and effective mothers. Both of whom know the place and power of humor. Good for them!

Family humor is not only powerful when facing death. It can also cloak an embarrassing moment or mask dumb decisions—all the while making an important point. A great humorist-mother wrote:

> *Our family would often go to a movie on Friday nights. On one of the Friday outings it was my turn to choose the movie we would go to. Though I had seen the previews, it turned out to be an unsuitable family movie. We no sooner were seated than it was evident I was WRONG. I suggested we leave but was overruled. That night has been known in our family as "the night mother blew it."*

Can you imagine how many times that story will be told in the passing of the years, probably with fascinating embellishments! Can you hear the laughter? *Family* laughter. The best telling of that tale will be at her wake as the family remembers the impact and value of an effective mother and then laughs—through their tears.

Just to make sure I had my head together at this point, I read that last excerpt to two large groups of teenagers, one of nearly 3,000 and the other 1,000+. Both groups responded the same way, especially at the writer's self-deprecating descriptive, "the night mother blew it." They laughed. When I asked some of them why they laughed, they all gave the same answer. They said the story reminded them about a similar experience in their own families. It struck a responsive chord. Good humor does that.

There are so many humorous possibilities in life. Some of life's better moments start out as fun, turn to frustration, and then flip back to fun again. An Illinois mother remembers:

Things aren't always the way you plan. I decided to take the family downtown in Chicago for lunch and a look at the Christmas decorations. It was planned as fun. Hardly had we gotten there—after the hassle of getting them all dressed, piled into the car, and downtown—before they started asking, "Can we go home now?" And they kept asking that question. All the while I, who had planned all this with such keen anticipation and high expectation weeks before, was thinking, "This is not the way it's supposed to be!" Some things work. Some things don't. Stay positive and keep your sense of humor. I can laugh now.

I specifically questioned young parents about the place of humor in their lives. They affirmed its importance. Would you have expected less? Following up on their answer, I asked them to share a humorous story with me. They did. No, they didn't. They told me stories, most of which weren't very funny. All had to do with cute things the children said or did or embarrassing things that happened to the parents because of their children. Neither translates well into the domain of public hilarity. The stories weren't funny to me because they were about very private things that happened to them. Anyone might laugh if he were there or knew the storyteller. But no professional comedian could make a living using the stories they told, not without a lot of massaging. Actually stories the young parents told were more like verbal home movies. Like home movies, they are of greatest interest to the people who took them or those who are on the screen.

When I had reached that conclusion, my curiosity was really stirred. If humor is such a wispy and vague thing, why the repeated mention of humor and laughter with so few hilarious examples? There had to be something more than I have mentioned so far. I reread all the letters and reviewed all the interview notes looking for answers. I was confident that one or more of these effective parents had clarified this issue but that I had missed their point. I was right. I had. And they had. Actually four had.

A lady from Indiana offhandedly commented: *Laughter brings happiness and helps a family become more open-minded. It also helps to laugh when you are under stress and facing tough times. It makes you feel like you can do anything.*

Wow! More than just a relief valve, our Indiana friend claims that laughter, and the humor that stirs it, refocuses and expands human energy. It's more than a diversion. Laughter gives a different slant to any problem and expands the range of a person's potential for dealing with it.

So, laugh when faced with stress! It's not an act of senseless bravado. In the hands of positive people it's an expression of hope and confidence. A Christian's laughter in the face of Satan can be a prayer and a way of expressing trust in God. Effective parents support that conclusion.

The daughter of effective California parents offers yet another insight on humor and laughter.

A sense of humor has provided a lot of the glue that holds us together as family. The Lord gave my dad a wonderful sense of humor with my mom having an equally special one—just more subtle and less expected. My sister and I have inherited some of it with a little different spin. I know that making people laugh, or at least smile, is very important to me. There's much, too much, grumpiness in the world. Any attempts to alleviate it are good. When you see the funny side of a situation it diffuses anger, hurt, and frustration. Our family laughs a lot with each other. Rarely at each other.

Her point? Humor and laughter not only diffuse the negative but accent the positive. As her letter's message floated across my mind, the oddest thing happened. Song titles, bits of poetry, and challenging quotes that had the same message stole up from my subconscious. "You've got to accentuate the positive," "Laugh and the world laughs with you; cry and you cry alone," "Smiling through the tears." Those are a few that bubbled up. You too?

A third twist on laughter and humor was offered by an Iowa father.

Our sense of humor has seen us through many awkward situations and has drawn us together. There have been times when life has gotten so very complicated and the absurdity of our situation so overwhelming that all we could do was laugh. That cleared the air and helped us get on with living.

That man sees laughter as a way of getting rid of life's confusion and dumping its useless debris. He believes that, like a dentist's drill cleans out decay so that solid reconstruction can happen, humor and laughter root out the unstable parts of life, making way for the future.

A fourth insight to the power and purpose of humor and laughter comes from a Louisiana mother who explains that laughter and humor give the family a different and better perspective of itself.

Humor is an important facet of our family. It starts with being able to laugh at ourselves. Then we try to find humor in whatever situation we are in. Teasing and joking around in a loving way are part of our daily life. We look for the positive side of situations, keeping in mind that God has our life planned for us.

As I wound my way through the writing of this chapter, I often found myself thinking about St. Paul and, especially, his letter to the Philippians. Even though it was written under such sour circumstances, many call it "The Epistle of Joy." He was in prison as he wrote that exuberant letter, upbeat and full of words like "joy" and "rejoicing." In the midst of all that horror, Paul found what he was looking for. Effective parents are like Paul. They, too, find humor, laughter, and the positive side in so many of life's poorer experiences. I remember a popular poster from the '60s: "If life gives you lemons—make lemonade." Effective families do just that, and then they laugh aloud—at and with each other—as they gulp down glass after glass after glass. Here's to humor, and laughter, and fun!

By the way, is there anything more lemonlike than that R-word: responsibility? I mean home responsibilities, of course. They are grim to some—chores. Or duties, pronouncing the word, do-o-o-o-ties. Some call them tasks. Whatever you call them, effective parents are convinced that children need to know about those words. How do I know this? Read on.

Aunt Becky Lives

◆

No matter how young they are, give your children the opportunity to help with chores. It may be harder for you to let them assist but it gives them a sense of self-worth. As an elderly lady once told me, "Even when it's easier to do it yourself, let them do it. It instills in them a desire to help after they've grown."

—A Minnesota Father

My daughter has helped with the chores since she was two-and-a-half years old. We live in a neighborhood with many elderly people. She has helped them, taking out their trash, mowing their lawns, walking their pets, and the like.

—An Ohio Single Mother

In one of the great scenes of the book, Tom Sawyer connives his friends into whitewashing his aunt's fence. Behind that scene stands the presence of Aunt Becky, his guardian, who believed in chores for children. Tom evaded the lesson she intended to teach but the lesson was there, nonetheless.

If Aunt Becky were alive today, she would have at least one qualification for parental effectiveness. Effective parents believe with a passion that children ought to have chores and be given responsibilities if they are to grow up right. They further believe that it's the parent's task to make sure both are doled out. They are convinced their sons and daughters can be taught, and must learn, responsibility. That's no small task according to this mother:

Organizing this rather large family into a smoothly operating unit has been quite a challenge to us. In the beginning of our blended family we had to set rules and regulations that were unfamiliar to all the children. It has taken a lot of effort to help the children learn and follow the guidelines. But we are getting to the point where the children know what is expected of them and for the most part function quite nicely.

They function nicely, "for the most part," she says, describing the what and why of household chores in a "yours and mine" family that is trying to become an "our" family. That's a tough environment in which to teach, but teach they do!

A Washington mother adds texture to the task of teaching responsibility.

For several reasons, Ron and I agree that the children should have chores. For one, these assignments will help the children learn a lesson of how to get a job done, and done properly. Number 2, we feel that the children, as members of the family, have a responsibility to help the family function as efficiently as possible.

Like those reasons for assigning chores? I do. But there's more to her understanding of what needs to happen in their home. She continues:

Number 3, there's no way I can handle the work load myself. So the children load the dishwasher, set and clear the table (including wiping down the counter tops and putting the food away), empty the dishwasher and put the dishes away, take the trash out daily, sweep the kitchen morning and evening, sweep the dining room and bathrooms, and feed the animals. Those chores are done on a weekly rotating basis. The children also keep their own rooms clean, which includes dusting and vacuuming every Saturday morning before the television can come on.

Whew! Her table of duties wears me out.

At first I thought this mother was an exception—a tough cookie. But effective home after effective home reported the same approach. There is total agreement among effective parents that children need to do meaningful work around the house. The specific assignments vary, but not the fact that assignments are made. An Arkansas mother recites the facts of life in her home. She and her husband have discovered:

> *Three children mean constant chaos, noise, and confusion. We insist that they do chores to help around the house. We involve them in our simpler daily activities, such as gardening.*

A Michigan mother adds: *Mike and I are big on teaching the girls responsibility. They wash cars and mow grass and clean the house. We work with them—lest we sound too harsh.*

They even give reasons for these assignments. Effective parents, great teachers that they are, see chores as lessons of their school-in-the-home. An Indiana mother says:

> *As the girls grew older they were given responsibilities. First, it was picking up their toys. Then making their beds, taking out the garbage, and feeding the pets. Every now and then we all had a special family work day. The girls would moan and groan, telling us none of their friends had to do this. They learned complaining would not get the work done so they might as well do their part. All three girls earned part of their spending money in high school and before.*

That paragraph needs to be massaged for its multiple insights into how effective parenting teaches responsibility. I easily pick out half a dozen. The first three interlock. (1) Tasks ought be age related, (2) This kind of teaching should start early in a child's life, (3) Life's first chores should be aimed at taking care of your own things.

Young parents concurred with this opening trio. They agree that early effort should be made at training the child toward basic responsibilities—such as picking up their own toys and putting the crayons back. As a parent you ought to have a toy box in which the toys can be easily dumped. Nothing ornate or costly. It can be just that: a box. The child can put things into a box. And crayons can be loaded into a coffee can or any kind of larger canister. Little hands have trouble doing tiny things, but they are great for picking up big crayons, big trains, big dolls, and big books and then dropping them into a big box or a big can. It's even a great way to first work the larger muscles and then, in time, the smaller ones.

As the child gets older, effective parents keep working with them. The slightly older task is aimed at bringing some minimum of order into their chores. Teach them to put the books together on a big shelf and the blocks into a separate box. The age at which you do this is more related to your child than it is to a specific date. Within the beginnings of life, responsibility must be taught.

But how? Let's go back to the list for two more suggestions: (4) Do things together as a family, (5) Let no one be excused from participation. What that means is that you don't have to wait until your daughter is strong enough to mow the lawn or your son is nimble fingered enough to help with the dishes to implement numbers 4 and 5. Put an apron on your son or daughter as you bake. Or give them a small rake to scratch around when you garden or mow. Yes, it's easier doing work without your child under foot. But the teaching is best done that way.

There are more insights from effective parents about the value of work, including: (6) Earning money and in so doing establish early the positive relationship between doing work and earning money.

A California dad came at number 6 by writing:

We strongly believe we should not give the children everything they ask for. They need to be taught value ... and the relationship between work and money. They have specific jobs around the house which are their responsibilities as family members. They get no pay for that but there are extra things they can do to earn money for things they want to buy.

That's a sophisticated approach to work, chores, family responsibility, and money. He uses money as an intentional incentive at home, but only after the basic responsibilities have been met.

A Minnesota mother tells how money comes into play in their effective family.

Our girls have always had responsibilities and jobs. They began early to save money— one fourth of all they earned. It really helped teach them the value of saving. Today they all handle savings and jobs in a way that makes parents proud.

When dealing with the tiny ones, it's too early to tie money and responsibility, but it's not too early to have a family plan and to sow the first seeds of linking work, responsibility, and money together. It's one of life's most important lessons. A Washington, D.C. congregation, adjacent to the Domestic Court, was asked to work with couples who were at the edge of divorce. Can you guess what they surfaced as the most common problem gnawing away at marital harmony? It was mishandling money and failing to understand the importance of proper money management. Effective parents start early at eliminating the mismanaged money problems from their children's later lives. They take the long view. Do the same yourself.

But lessons about money are still not the whole of teaching the importance of work. There is a value in the work itself, whether it generates income or not. Two parents, one from Florida and one from Texas, underline that point.

- *Our children were expected to keep their rooms tidy, pick up their clothes, and be help-ful—the same as we expect of our-selves. Although we didn't assign a lot of day-to-day tasks, there was always Saturday. On Saturday all six of us pitched in to do yard work. We did the work faster if any one had plans for later in the day. Parents often plan work around their time and needs and disregard the kids' time and needs. That seemed unfair to us. We thought the kids should be considered too. All the kids did odd jobs in the summer, but no one worked during the school year. If they were desperate for money, we'd come up with a task to earn a few dollars such as clean the bathroom shower tile, a job we all hated.*

(Just for fun, count how often "we" appears—and note the thought to which each mention is attached.)

- *When there's a project to be done at home, everyone pitches in. Our children have learned home repairs, remodeling, gardening, and many other things that we feel are sur-vival skills. We believe they learned that work could be fun too. In addition, they see their contribution is important to our family.*

Are there benefits for teaching responsibility to children? Read almost any newspaper on any day. Today's carried the story of a mother who had lapsed into a diabetic coma while at home with her four-year-old child. When the little boy realized what was happening (he had been told what could occur), he tried to give his mother sugar, as he had been taught. That didn't seem to work, so he called 911 and gave exact directions to his home. More: He did not open the door for the medics until he was sure who they were. Quite a story! Why had he known what to do? He had been taught by a mother who had told the little tyke what to do if she passed out. That was today's story. Tomorrow's will be just as exciting! You'll be amazed by what some little children do—because someone believed they could and should be given responsibility.

Where does that happen best? At home, of course. Task, duty, and responsibility must be part of the core curriculum in any school-at-home. Effective parents believe that responsibility is best taught in the home by parents who work side by side with their children. It took me a while to understand that parental work expectations are not excessive. They make work at home teamwork—and start it early. Children whose parents believe work and responsibilities are important get a great head start on life.

Head start on life? Every child deserves one and gets it in effective families. Giving that kind of a head start is what the next chapter is all about. You won't want to miss it. In many ways it's the best in this book. See if you agree.

Forgive,
It's the Only Way to Forget

The miracle of forgiveness practiced on a daily basis makes it possible for us to live together and love each other sacrificially. My husband and I grew up in families of forgiveness and acceptance.

—An Illinois Wife

When Jim and I get in the way of God's love working in and through us (that means we sin), we are able to go to God for help and forgiveness. Through His forgiveness and help we are able to forgive each other continually. Forgiveness! It's very important because we fail all the time.

—A Maryland Mother

I am a failure in so many ways. I pray that only God and I see that. When my wife and son see that, I pray that they will forgive. I need help. Maybe that's why I teach a parent Sunday school class on family subjects. I help myself as I try to help others.

—A Wisconsin Father

For much of my life I thought the synonym for "forgive" was "forget." Yet, try as I would, long after I thought I had forgiven someone else—or myself—I remembered. What? The thing I kept telling myself I had forgotten. I kept confusing the old saying: "To err is human, to forgive is divine" assuming that since I was such an expert in the erring, I could be just as accomplished at forgiving. Wrong.

Wherein was my mistake? I forgot that forgiving is not something I do. God does that for me through Jesus Christ. I have no forgiving power. That biblical concept of forgiving means, "cover over," "send away," or "let go." I can't do any of that. Neither can anyone else—not even an effective parent. Only God can forgive.

Even so, it came as somewhat of a surprise that effective parents' most vigorous and vehement convictions were reserved for the subject of this chapter: forgiveness. Do they ever have opinions! By the time effective parents are done with the subject of forgiveness, they have intertwined with it every other subject in this book—from communication to humor to the power of touch. For example, remembering his roots and those of his wife, a Nebraska dad tells how his present practice of forgiveness interconnects with his past, saying:

We never seem to have the knock-down-drag-out fights that our friends experience. We realize that our childhood programming was responsible for that. We were raised to adhere to the Scriptural admonition of not letting the sun go down on our wrath. We love each other and just won't go to sleep if there is hostility between us. We were raised that way by committed parents.

In his five sentences about forgiveness there are three references to family roots—an important subject in this book. See how it works?

Others also turned back in time as they discussed forgiveness, only not so far. A Texas mother remembers her dating days:

When we were courting, Don wouldn't leave if one of us was angry with the other because his mother had told him, "Do not let the sun go down while you are still angry" (Eph. 4:26). I remember nights when he'd sit by the hour in the hallway, just inside the doorway to my apartment, being quiet so as not to wake my roommate. We'd had some argument. I just wanted him to leave. But he wouldn't. We'd talk and talk until we finally worked things out so neither of us would go to bed angry.

In Iowa they look back and remember too. Note the insight into how forgiveness and forgetting interact as this father slips into his last line.

My most vivid memory as a father is when I spanked Tim for being disobedient. But I had acted in haste. Tim was not at fault.

When I realized this, I did the only thing I could. I asked him for forgiveness. I reminded him that as his earthly father I made mistakes, but his heavenly Father loved him and never made mistakes. This nine-year-old boy, through his sobs, gave me his forgiveness. In his prayers that night he offered me forgiveness again. I have never forgotten that incident. Strangely, my now 26-year-old son does not remember it at all.

Do you have any idea why that son does not remember his father's sin? I have. I think the son forgave him. Has the father not forgiven himself? Has he not yet dumped his shame at the foot of the cross and left it there? An Indiana mother has:

I'm not the world's greatest housekeeper. Our home more often resembles a workshop than "Better Homes and Gardens." The one kind of housework I insist upon is tending relationships. We don't always agree, but we don't let the infractions of the day drive long-lasting wedges into relationships. Forgiveness is the lowest common denominator. When someone's sins show, that is no surprise. We don't harp on each other's sinfulness. We acknowledge that God's diagnosis is right on. We've got the problem. God has the solution. We need to focus on the cure which is God's love and power in Jesus.

Let me repeat. The writers of the last two excerpts—and so many others throughout the book—are not trained theologians. They are effective Christian parents. They write as they do because their lives are tuned to the heart of God, who through His Word speaks to their own deepest needs.

With that as background let's listen to others who wrote about forgiveness and its application to marriage and family. I'll begin with a little commentary on defensiveness. Very little. To wit, effective parents aren't very defensive. They easily admit doing wrong. They quickly confess their sin—and seek forgiveness. An Arizona dad states it Arizona-clear:

> *God is the important part of our life. He better be. As people we are not perfect. We need forgiveness for our sins. We also need to forgive each other.*

This Arizona father has a spiritual twin in Ohio who echoes his sentiment, but moves the discussion a few paces further down the road. For the Ohio father, forgiveness is a way for keeping his defensiveness in check.

> *We have our share of arguments and disagreements. When conflict arises, we try to talk things out after everyone has cooled off. Having a time apart works best for letting everyone cool off. Then can come forgiveness.*

Not only does that Ohio man understand the importance of forgiveness, but he also understands some of the process that helps forgiveness happen.

And what stirs up forgiveness in effective families? They are nearly unanimous on the answer to that question: Talking together stirs up forgiveness and helps it happen best. An Iowa mom tells:

> *When we as parents have wronged one of the children, we go to them. We confess our wrong, apologize, ask for—and then receive—forgiveness. We then talk it all over with the whole family and together pray to God, asking forgiveness.*

If you divide up that Iowa mother's commentary, a six-step approach to forgiveness emerges. (1) Go to the one offended. (2) Confess the wrong. (3) Apologize. (4) Ask for their forgiveness. (5) Accept the forgiveness offered. (6) Discuss what had happened with the entire family so that it won't happen again. Maybe. Whatever the possibility of recurrence, her process breathes the spirit, and the letter, of the Gospels. Dig around in Matthew 18 and elsewhere. It's all there!

But who goes through all that? Effective families do. They go through those steps because they understand the importance of forgiveness for themselves—and for their family's health.

Just so you don't think our Iowa mother is an oddity, I'll let four more parental forgiveness-specialists check in. If I had the space, I would present more. Of the four, two live above the Mason-Dixon Line and two below. The importance and practice of forgiveness isn't regional.

- *We admit our mistakes to our children. We let them know when something we did is wrong. We tell them we are sorry and ask for their forgiveness—and God's.*

- *Leo and I are far from being perfect parents and we believe that it is important to admit to our children when we have blown it. We ask for forgiveness for our wrong behavior.*

- *I try to yield to Jim's wishes. He is never unreasonable with our daughter or with me. We've had a few spats—I can't remember a major argument. When we do have a tiff, one of us always asks for forgiveness very quickly. We talk about it, usually briefly. The other person says, "That's okay," and we let it go.*

- *Yes, we do argue now and then. But all families do. We have learned to apologize and sincerely mean it. We hug and kiss and say we are sorry to each other. Then we can forgive and forget.*

As you walked through those four reports, didn't certain words and phrases surface? I mean words such as "admit," "let them know," "tell," "ask," "talk," "say," "apologize." Those words encourage openness during the confession process and stir up a readiness to grant forgiveness once the confessing is over. Right? Added together they teach us that we need to say we are wrong when that's the case and then we need to say that we are sorry. After that the other needs to say the forgiving words. Out loud. Right? None of that why-should-I-say-things-out-loud-they-know-how-I-feel. No strong silent stuff. Effective families spill out their mistakes and hunger to hear the responding forgiveness offered in response. Clearly.

Can parents help? They sure can. My own dear mother had a sure way to settle forgiveness questions. First came the confession and the request for forgiveness. Then came the acceptance—out loud. Then came THE KISS! Yes, a kiss. You can't imagine how sour a face can look until a brother or sister comes at you with a reluctant pucker to which you have to respond in kind. The laughter! The touching! The forgiveness! Even the smallest ones can forgive and can learn how to accept forgiveness.

But not all forgive well. Some can't seem to do it at all. What happens then? One man offers this tale.

My wife and I do not communicate for a number of reasons. Sounds ominous. Any hope to work forgiveness into their relationship? However, we are so committed and bound to faithfulness in marriage that we just keep on forgiving and accepting one another—all by God's grace in Christ.

What a comfort his story brings! Forgiveness can even happen in the lives of those who can't get all the parts working right. The reason forgiveness works for them is that they have introduced a third party into their awkward relationship: Jesus Christ. He brings just what they need, His special gift of forgiveness.

Any word for others of us in the same fix? I'll let a Kansas husband answer.

Being married 19 years means we have been willing to change along the way. I'm grateful that the changes our family has experienced have all been in the direction of a closer walk with the Lord. With the drive to change always comes the power to be forgiving of one another.

Bumblers can hope to change because forgiveness in and through the Savior lubricates the forgiving process and becomes its continuous product too.

When some effective parents write about the important things in their lives, their words sound as if they are copying pages from the Bible. With inspired words a mother encourages God's people to change whatever needs changing in their homes and families—and then tells us how that changing can happen. See if you agree.

Keep Christ in the center of your home. In everything you do or say or think, allow the Holy Spirit to guide you. Live always in joy, confident of your salvation. Forgive as God forgives you. Be a "pipeline" for Jesus, allowing His love to flow through you to others. Don't be discouraged when you make a mistake and mess up. Fix it or forget it. God does.

With those words she has captured the spirit of Scripture, including her conclusion, "Fix it or forget it." Most things are fixable. We may not be able to return them to their original condition, but they are fixable. Then pray for divine power to do a divine thing: forget it. My only addition to her paragraph is replacing a good two-letter word with a better three-letter one. Instead of, "Fix it or forget it," I would say, "Fix it and forget it."

Is that possible? Here's testimony from Ohio as to the "how" of fixing and forgetting:

Ours is not a perfect family. We get angry with each other. We suffer through illnesses and injuries. We live through disappointments, have frustrations that bother us to the core, and sometimes we just do dumb things. But we work through all these weaknesses by keeping a close relationship with the Lord, supporting each other, worshiping regularly, and living not just for ourselves but for others as well.

What if the sin is concrete, painful, pervasive ... and public? What then? Is it fixable and forgettable then? Listen to this Minnesota mother and decide for yourself.

I think forgiveness played a large part in the survival of our extended family. When my husband's crime came to light, there were members of the family who expected me to divorce him. They were victims of his misdealing. I didn't divorce him. Their understanding took time. But when they saw I could forgive the pain, embarrassment, and resulting hardship he brought to me, they, too, found their hearts softened and felt the healing balm of forgiveness.

Who felt the balm of forgiveness? Who was healed? Who? For the answer, read that effective mother's commentary again.

How shall we wrap up this chapter? I'll let an effective Indiana dad do it. In his letter he ties together so many of the themes effective parents have put forth.

Through all these years and in all the places we have lived, we have been actively involved in church life and have tried to keep Christ at the center and as the head of our household. Of course, not without forgettings and forgivings. We were very young when we married and had our children. We depended on our God and on our parents who taught us His love through our own growing years.

When I first outlined this book, the next, and last, chapter was the first one. That was okay, but the longer I dealt with the letters the more that chapter's theme seemed to fit better as a conclusion than as an introduction. We need to remember the wonderful variety of effective families. Otherwise, as one parent wrote, *we'll act as if families can be cookie-cuttered.* They can't. They come in all kinds of shapes. Some of them aren't even "cookies!" To press the metaphor a little harder, some of them are hardly into the dough level of family life, while others are already day-old. But dough or day-old, they are family and have within themselves the potential for effectiveness.

The Many Faces of Effectiveness

Perfection is not a descriptive family word.
—A Michigan Father

I thought I was going to grow up, work a few years, and then stay home and raise a family like my mom. Boy, was I wrong.
—An Illinois Mother

Tell me. What, exactly, should effective parents look like? And their families? Together, are they updates of the 1950s average of Mom, Dad, and 1.4 children? Yes. No. Sometimes.

These effective husbands and wives who shape their children toward the 21st century, are they always available, ever sensitive and super ready? Yes. No. Sometimes.

Are they even a "they?" Is there such a thing as a single effective parent? Yes. No. Sometimes.

By now you must know the truth. No matter how you come at effective parents or effective parenting, there are no easy answers, no single model.

Answers. Models. Always in the plural. Effectiveness has many faces. Many. It actually has as many faces as there are effective parents.

Some are unbelievably neat and tidy. All-American. Scrubbed. That's the way they are. Some, anyway. They work hard on their public image and on their family appearance. It shows. Their homes could be the set for "Father Knows Best" or "Leave It to Beaver." The owners are effective—and they just happen to keep their houses that way.

Another snapshot of effectiveness is the self-portrait of a Californian who through most of his life reported his family was *secure and middle class in their life-style*. Then the unthinkable happened. He was laid off and the photo blurred. Or did it clear up? *We are now living on our good credit history, trying to race the clock against bankruptcy*. That's how some effectiveness looks. Some of the time.

Most of those I heard from—meaning more than half—are middle-class Americans. They ought to be. So are most families in our country. That's what middle class means. As such they own their homes (mortgaged, of course), have jobs (sometimes more than one), and bring in enough money to live on (most weeks). Their repeated comment, usually just dropped into a paragraph here or there, is that while they work hard and save regularly for the things they have, they feel wonderfully blessed by God. That's how it is—with some. They work hard. They save regularly. They trust God.

More? As hard as they work, most are not much into materialism. Acquiring the signs of success, which drove the American economy during the '60s, '70s, and '80s, is not their bag. They have other uses for money: family vacations, family recreation, family educational goals. Some couples determined their life-style when they were courting. Some even before. Some decided that having children was a planned benefit. Almost all seem satisfied with life, have an inner peace, and are content. There's not much energy in this group for getting way ahead in life. They have other more pressing priorities.

You ought to know that there are no poverty-level parents in this study. While some of those who report are poorer and work hard making things stretch, there are no homeless, no poverty-level folk. I made no attempt to avoid them. They just didn't surface. Was that because the really poor are so busy surviving that they haven't time to talk about the effective parenting many are doing? Maybe. I know from experience that there are some great moms and dads in all economic classes.

Wrenching poverty aside, these pages still overflow with real life on an awesome scale. Effective families are not spared pain, suffering, and heartache. They, too, are called to face life's toughest moments and endure its cruelest blows. Listen to this effective mother and see if I am not right.

We are what is known as a blended family. My husband and I found ourselves single again under two different sets of circumstances. After remaining steadfast and committed to his marriage for more than 10 years, he discovered his wife was seeking companionship and support from another. Two years later she divorced him, leaving the children in his custody, and remarried. He felt he could never love openly and without hesitation again. God had other plans. Twelve miles away I was going through my own life-altering crisis. My first husband and daughter were involved in a head on collision that killed him instantly and left her hospitalized and paralyzed. In an instant I went from a happily married mother of three healthy children to a widow and single mother of one very critically injured child and her younger brother and sister. Ten months later my injured daughter died. But God continued, as He had been since the accident, to provide the help and support I needed. I felt I could never love another as I had. But God had other plans.

I chose to begin with that history of effectiveness because current studies project that half or more of all teenagers will spend some significant part of their teen years in a blended family. This specific family is dealing with blending that flows from two sources: death and divorce. Yet theirs is a face of effectiveness.

Another gripping chronicle:

Four years ago I was diagnosed with breast cancer. I have had intensive chemotherapy and radiation, a double mastectomy, and numerous biopsies. The cancer has recurred. It has been a tough four years, but we have survived. Many beautiful events have helped us, and we have learned fundamental truths.

Her full report is a record of travail and triumph that is not finished as I write this. It is still spinning its way toward a conclusion. Her commitment to confront cancer is not the reason I quote her. It's her commitment to confront cancer while continuing to work at parental effectiveness—a spirit as much her husband's as hers—that qualifies both of them for recognition as effective parents. What a couple!

That kind of letter—sometimes involving a husband and other times a wife, sometimes telling of an accident, sometimes reporting a tragic incident, sometimes relating how an effective family handled an awesome disease—came in by the dozens. How do effective parents handle life's brutalizing blows? Lots of ways. They laugh. They cry. They support. They love. They keep on effective familying and parenting. Get it clear: Effective families are not effective because they are unscathed, as Satan asserted in Job 2:4–5. They are scathed—badly so—but they are still effective.

A couple more snapshots of real life? This is written by the teenage daughter of an effective blended parental pair:

> *I'm Jenny, the middle child—the peanut butter and jelly in a PBJ sandwich. My parents are divorced and both have remarried. I live with my mom and stepdad, though he's not really my stepdad. He's just Dad. I don't think I could call him by his first name any more than I could call my granny Marian. Here, with my mom, I have a younger sister (stepsister) and older brother (full brother).*

This young lady knows, loves, and visits with her natural father. She exists in two worlds, helped in the process by four parents, all of whom she sees as effective. Different—but effective. Her situation is not ideal. But the parents and Jenny will not give up on their quest for the best expression of effectiveness they can achieve.

Some great effective parents aren't even parents. They are parent. One:

> *My husband died after 28 years of marriage. At that time one son was 15 and the other four. You can see I had to do much for myself.*

Parenting alone is tougher and requires more adaptability and inventiveness than doing so as a pair. But it clearly can be done. If that's your calling, don't give up. Single parents can be, and are, effective.

I have three more "stories." Each shows another face of parental effectiveness. Maybe one is like yours.

- *A big change occurred when my second cousin was killed in an accident leaving four fatherless children without a mother. I didn't know her well but we took in her children. After a series of events we were able to keep two with us. We have been richly blessed by their presence in our family, and as we grow closer through this experience, we realize God's plan for us was to open our hearts and home to these four wonderful children. Had I not quit my full-time career a year earlier, I would not have offered even temporary shel-ter to these parentless kids. A grand design is evident in all this and we thank God for allowing us to parent in this extended way. In many ways my husband's background prepared us for this event. He had experienced first hand, as a young man, what being an orphan meant. We try to get all my second cousin's four children together whenever possible. We probably qualify as an extended family—but in a non-traditional way.*

- I cried when I read this wonderful letter from an effective mother. *Let me apologize for not writing sooner. I have been busy and have to keep busy. I lost my son 15 months ago. It is hard coping with the loss. But God has blessed me and helps me each day. My son, who was killed, had finished junior college and would have finished college in May. The devil jumped into a young man and he killed my son. That was my Mother's Day gift in 1990. But, you know, my son had cleaned the storage building and bought my Mother's Day gift the day of the night he was killed. He was taken from me, but he was baptized and grew up in the church. I thank God for all these blessings. When you lose a 22-year-old son, it hurts. Through prayer, my church family, friends, and family, I will survive.*

- The story of an effective trio: mom, dad, and daughter. *We are blessed with our beautiful Elizabeth who has Neurofibromatosis—the disease of the Elephant Man. Not only does Elizabeth have NF but it is moderately severe. She has a large tumor on the right side of her face, cheek, eyelid, and temple and the sight in her right eye is almost gone. She has had six surgeries in her short life. She has had to learn to deal with stares, comments, and questions. We try not to make the people who stare or ask questions feel bad or defensive. Most people are just curious. Experiencing this helped me collaborate on a pamphlet "What to Say When People Stare." I pray daily that I can be the kind of parent God wants me to be for this special child. [I pray to be] the kind of parent she needs to guide her, support her, help her develop, and become the kind of well-adjusted person who has a lot to contribute to others. We have tried to emphasize her inner qualities. She is beautiful on the inside and has a charisma like you wouldn't believe, an outgoing personality, and can cope with life's punches.*

This book is written by people like that. I believe an effective parent's heart beats in all their letters and comments. The specifics I have cited are on the edges of the average. I cite them to give you a sweep and a sense of the size of effective parenting. Even when the examples lack this kind of drama, all effective parents have burdens, different only in scale from one another. All have problems. What makes them different from other parents is how they handle their problems.

One more important observation: No effective parents even hinted that they wished they were problemless. Many wished they were more skilled in handling the problems they have. But once their load becomes obvious, effective parents seem to reorient their life's compass toward dealing with reality rather than complaining. I concluded that effective parents are realists. They don't let crises paralyze their effectiveness. Crises stir them to creative action.

Example? Remember our west coaster who had been laid off when he was well on in life? So what do you think he and his family made out of that disaster? Let me repeat a part of his letter, which we've read before:

> We've developed a strong faith over the years and God has truly sustained us. The past two years have helped the whole family open up and trust in God's guidance in our lives. We've dropped out of our very secure middle-class life-style, but have stepped up into a far more secure Christian faith. I can't tell you how much our kids (and their parents) have grown in their faith through all this unemployment and financial hardship.

Excerpts from effective families' letters and comments have woven life into this book. I have edited and abbreviated material, but I have not altered their clear meaning. In a few instances I added a clarifying word or modified a verb tense for clarity. I also masked beyond detection circumstances that were personal and private, either in my opinion or the sources'.

As example of all this, I share with you words from an effective parent who was not able to fully participate in this exploration. He/she wrote but once, asking that his/her specific location and circumstance not be revealed. But he/she wanted us to see another face of effective parenting—the face of one who serves on with no evidence of success to encourage his/her continued faithfulness. The letter was written so that I (you and I?) might be led *to look beyond the typical family and see the needs of God's other children.*

And his/her story? They had opened their home, already blessed with at least one natural child, to other children in desperate circumstances—children who were starting out life at a great disadvantage. He/she told me:

> *At this point I am trying to deal with the fact that what I consider a healthy productive life may not be possible for any of them. Most of their problems were caused by drug use of their parents and by the abuse they suffered in their earlier homes. The pain I deal with daily nearly blinds me to all the blessings that God has bestowed on us during the journey. We may have grown from the experience, but our children appear to be headed for lives that definitely won't parallel ours. Nothing on the market today assists parents with children like ours. I have had to come to terms with the idea that success in parenting for us must be defined*

as doing one's reasonable best no matter what the results.

This effective parent adds:

What you have to understand, yet so few seem to, is that we love these children as much as any parent loves their kids. Their pain is our pain. They were taught of God's love from the time they entered our lives. It was not enough. I realize the results are not in yet—and that parents with normal children have no guarantees—but it is hard keeping our spirits up.

Effective parent that he/she is, the writer finishes with a gift for parents, effective or not, everywhere.

There is probably only one thing I can share with other parents. I would tell them not to hide from any problems that their children seem to have. Work diligently to find help for them. So many people have assisted us. But we had to look hard to find them.

Many faces. Just as many faces of parents with children under four. How is it with them? Same song, second stanza. They look like their older brothers and sisters.

For a change of pace I'll start with a less-than-common, but not all that uncommon face: This is our first baby and we do not intend to have any more. The writer is not unhappy having a child or disturbed by the family situation. The two of them have decided to have only one child. Maybe. Maybe they'll even change their minds; maybe their best laid plans will go awry. They are not the only ones who say they want but one child. However, they are a minority. Most parents of the very young volunteered that they have their eye on child number 2, and maybe number 3.

More snapshots of younger parents? Here's a composite of what they are like on the subject of readiness to make parental judgements—and how they do that:

I follow my heart and do what I think best. I listen to and react to things with which I basically agree. I am the expert on how to father my children. Everyone will give you advice. I say listen to it, and then do what's right for you and your child. It's our job as a mom and dad to sort out the advice we receive. In the final analysis I trust my gut instinct.

While those younger parents are cautious about their capacity for parental judgement, they feel they are prepared to act responsibly. And why not? Many (not all) believe their parents were effective. For that reason they know what effectiveness looks like. In addition, most of them were deep into their twenties before that first child was born. While they were getting ready for their moment, they watched others carefully, matured in their understanding, set goals, and developed a pretty solid financial base.

They also know the identifying characteristics of an effective parent. That parent, they say:

[Is] one who exhibits love and makes the child a priority. There is a certain tired peace about them. One who, in a public situation, is constantly aware of the children. Effective parents show emotion with the family and revel in the bonding that results. They are tuned into their child's needs and try their best to meet them. They take their children seriously as human beings.

Are these younger parents spiritual?

I pray every day for my children. It's the parents' job to teach the child about God and set the example of a Christian life. With two under three years of age, we are really into forgiveness, showing how it's Jesus' forgiveness of us that makes it possible for us to forgive others. It is the platform of our beliefs. If the parents' world view includes a spiritual component, so will the child's.

So there you have it: some of the many faces of effectiveness. Don't give up if your parental face is not the same as another's. Instead take a close look at the different ways effectiveness shows itself. Let their witness reinforce the best in you. Let that witness stir you to change things that are inferior. Reinforce the one. Look for ways to improve the other. That's how effective parents do it.

Postscript:
More, More, and More

◆

This book actually has no ending. As I write the last sentences of this first book, I already have in hand material from which the second in this effective parenting series will grow. The first one was for parents of the youngest and they backed up what their older brothers and sisters wrote. I got it too! You've read what tomorrow's mature, effective parents have to say. Sounds to me like they are ready right now. But like everyone else, they will have to drive on down life's road a bit further before they know with certainty the certainty of what they know.

In the second book I will fall back, again, on the words and witness of effective parents. I have so many of their quotes in my file, unused. In addition I have a bundle of new letters to excerpt from. Some have come from those who could not make the earlier deadlines. Some are from new nominees. Some just wrote me when they heard what I was doing. I will harvest all those letters for insights.

May I also encourage you to write me? Send your insights and opinions to me in care of Concordia Publishing House, 3558 S. Jefferson Ave., St.

Louis, Missouri 63118-3968. If I can, I'll individually respond to your letters. If I can't do that, you may be assured I'll read what you wrote and use your offerings in the best way I am able.

With the next book I am turning to an additional source of understanding about effective families: school teachers. Who has a clearer view—a better seat at the family drama—than our classroom observers? I have asked many of them to help me help us all by sharing what they think parents ought to know about parenting children. I'm confident they will be a wonderful effective parenting resource. I ought to be. I have already heard from more than 200!

And then beyond that book is another on effective parenting and teens. That world has been open to me for years, and I've enjoyed every moment in it. How do I feel about the teens? I believe they face more testings of faith and life on any given morning of their life than I did in all my teen years. I love them. I admire them. I respect them. I listen to them.

There's one more voice in this series featuring effective parents. It will be a very unique parenting group—those whose children are grown and who, as such, are parents themselves. How do the older moms and dads parent those parents? I'm not sure, but I know who to ask. I'll ask them. I will.